Dear Aaron and Hur

for Brenda Salter McNeil

Dear Aaron and Hur

An intimate portrait of the life and times
of Julia Supple Andrus

HUGH STEVEN

Printed in the United States of America.

Unless otherwise noted, Scripture quotations are taken from the King James Version.

ISBN: 0-9769634-1-8

Cover design by Jewel Fink.
Interior design by Lee A. Steven

Library of Congress Cataloging-in-Publication Data is available.

Steven, Hugh.
    Dear Aaron and Hur /by Hugh Steven
    ISBN: 0-9769634-1-8
    Missionary, Bible translation, Biography, Autobiography, Memoirs.

*Dedicated to all the Aarons and Hurs
who have faithfully supported and prayed
for the ministry of Bible translation*

Julia Supple Andrus

Feb. 14, 1919 – Dec. 15, 2004

Maps of Mexico and the State of Chiapas

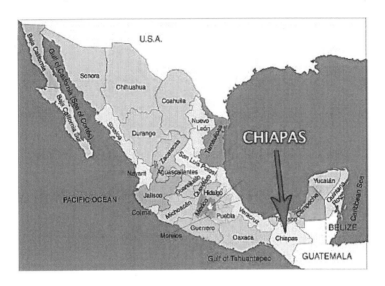

Contents

Introduction 1

Chapter One

On the Road Again, 1948 5

More Indian Trails 7
I Wish I Were an Indian 9
Thankful for Safety Pins 11
A Recipe for Translation 13

Chapter Two

Christmas in Mexico, 1951 15

Head Food 19
The Kingdom of Heaven Suffers Violence 21
Knee Work 23
Critical Days 24

Chapter Three

The Fellowship of His Suffering, 1952 27

Don't Forget the Lepers 29
A Trip to Las Margaritas 31
A Trip Deferred and Loves Knows What To Do 33
Prayer Is Not Water Spilled on the Ground 37
An Ordinary Day 38

Chapter Four

Faith as Real as Potatoes, 1953 – 54 40

Blessed To Be Among the Blessed 41

The Crossroad of a Million Private Lives 43
Faith Seeking Understanding 45
Out of the Mouth of Babes 46
A Macedonian Call 51
Group Service 53
Under Divine Orders 54

Chapter Five
Stateside, 1955 – 57 57
His Softest Whisper 57
Is There no End to His Comforts? 59
A Joy Letter 61
Our Gibraltar 67
Christmas Night, 1957 68
Puebla, Puebla 71
Join Wycliffe and See the World 74

Chapter Six
The Rainy Season, 1958 76
It Never Rains but it Pours 77
I'll Just Say Hello 81
Written from Corralito 87

Chapter Seven
Jungle Living, 1959 – 60 90
At Home in Santa María 90
Spiritual Battle in the Heavenlies 92
Annoyances 94
Translation Workshops 95

Chapter Eight
Living on Borrowed Time, 1961 – 64 115
    She Needs Much Prayer..................................117
    Rethinking My Life..124
    Asking Ultimate Questions 127
    Never Think God's Delays Are God's Denials...........128

Chapter Nine
A Half Century Letter, 1919 – 1969 133

Chapter Ten
Wearing Three Hats..147

Chapter Eleven
Plunking the First String 161

Chapter Twelve
It's Good To Be Married 172

Chapter Thirteen
The End of the Journey 185

Afterword
Outside Help..201

Acknowledgments...210
Appendix A: Idiomatic Translations 214
Appendix B: An Explanation of "Aaron and Hur" 217

Introduction

For more than a year, Wycliffe's archivist, Cal Hibbard, had been e-mailing to ask if I could do something with a series of newsletters written by Julia Supple. "They are unique," he told me. The letters had been sent to Cal from Julia's friend and colleague Ruth Bishop, who, after Julia's death, discovered the collection while cleaning out her apartment. With an appreciation for Julia's singular writing style, Ruth said: "These are too good to be tossed."

I had known Julia in Mexico and later when she worked in the home office of Wycliffe U.S.A, then headquartered in Huntington Beach, California. Whenever people spoke of her, the conversation inevitably turned to her *Dear Aaron and Hur* newsletters. And, without prompting, there was universal agreement that she was a clever wordsmith and a whimsical storyteller.

The morning I cleared my desk and began to read through her letters, which usually began with her signature salutation, *Dear Aaron and Hur,* I was impressed with a writing style that often read like her personal journal. In some respects, these were musings with herself as much as her news and musings for the people to whom she wrote. Although Julia's prose was often plainspoken, she had a lyrical spark that reflected a wit and playful humor that took nothing away from her thoughtful, often wise insights into the mystery of the Christian experience and her ongoing ministry among the Tojolabal people of Southern Mexico.

As I continued to organize the material and write her story, I realized her letters were short narrative gems. Many read like a short story. As one of Julia's colleagues has remarked: "Her letters were so fine, so memorable that I often smiled when I read them. She had the ability to transport you and make you see and feel her story of what it was like to live and work among ethnic people."

In many ways this is an old-fashioned story and perhaps out of step with Wycliffe's ministry in the 21st century. Computers, the Internet, television, iPhones and technology of all kinds have penetrated even the remotest village and hamlet in Mexico and, indeed, throughout the world. And, although Wycliffe's goal of Bible translation for ethnic peoples without the Scriptures remains steadfast, Wycliffe's methodology has changed to include national translators and partnerships with various mission agencies, such as the Reformed Church missionaries mentioned in some of the letters that follow. Certainly it is true that few, if any, of our current SIL (Summer Institute of Linguistics) workers in Mexico or elsewhere are required to ride hours

on horseback to reach their village allocation as Julia
regularly did.

My role within Wycliffe has been that of an historical
biographer and I found in Julia's story what I and others
believe should be preserved: a candid, dramatic picture of
pioneer Bible translation in rural Mexico during a period of
Wycliffe's early history. Yet, this story is much more than
an historical artifact. It is a compelling human drama that
transcends time. Julia's newsletters constitute a kind of
devotional that allows the reader to identify with her self-
questioning, self-doubt and spiritual and physical resolve in
the midst of extremely difficult and sometimes impossible
conditions. It's also a love story, of marriage deferred and
regained, where Julia, on the eve of her engagement late in
life, said: "Take it from me, you can be just as excited about
a good man at age sixty as you can at twenty."

Julia's correspondence is free from cliché and overly
pious jargon and reveals a woman who could write playful
prose, who did not think too highly of herself, and yet who
took seriously her responsibility as a Bible translator. She
was in love with life, her Lord, the written Word and the
ministry God had given her. In her life's unexplained
disturbances, she often wrote: "I am not worried about
tomorrow, for I have seen yesterday and I love today."

The art of any memoir or biography is to show the reader
what is happening not only on the surface of a person's life,
but below and above and on the inside as well. What you
will find in the following letters to *Dear Aaron and Hur* is an

intimate portrait of the very human and endearing life and times of Julia Supple Andrus. You will be taken on a journey to a culture and time distant from our own, but you will recognize instantly and respond to the sparkling personality at the center of it all.

Hugh Steven
Santa Ana, California
August 2012

1

On the Road Again, 1948

Traveling in rural Mexico during the 1940s and 50s was to experience a reality far removed from the expectations of those who promoted "travel" as a charming way to discover new lands and cultures. When 23-year-old Julia Supple and most of her colleagues journeyed to the remote and isolated villages and ranches of Mexico's ethnic minorities, they most often experienced the original meaning of the word travel. From the old French word *travail* comes such meanings as "harsh," "trouble," "torment" and even "torture."

Writing in a style that became a legend among her Wycliffe colleagues and supporting partners, Julia's newsletters documented her many adventures, trials, disappointments, and small triumphs. Her letters were refreshingly free of missionary clichés and her prose reflected her good sense of humor, infused with witticisms, little jokes, jibes, and ironies of all kinds. Julia also had the striking ability to extract rich and provocative spiritual conclusions from her experiences.

In the very first of a long series of newsletters sent to family and her praying and supporting partners, we are treated to her feelings and understated humor as she leaves her regular assignment among the Tojolabal people in the State of Chiapas, Mexico, to take a difficult overland journey to the coastal village of Salina Cruz in the State of Oaxaca.

February 1948

Traveling on a second-class bus means chickens and squealing pigs, Indians and *serapes*, folks crowded into the aisle, either standing or crouched on the dirty floor. It means squirming and adjusting arms and legs to get a moment's sleep. It means bumping along rough roads and gazing on majestic, breath-taking scenery. It means being a real, living part of Mexican life.

Tomorrow morning I begin another trek southward, but to a different place. This time I'm going to a little coastal town called Salina Cruz on the Isthmus of Tehuantepec. Two days traveling from that point is a Chontal Indian village where two of my colleagues work—one of them, Mae Morrison, is ill and must be evacuated as soon as possible. Instead of going the usual way by horseback or ox cart or boat, we want to try and get an MAF[1] plane to land somewhere along the beach. While Mae is

---

[1] A Mission Aviation Fellowship airplane.

recuperating from her illness, my colleague, Vi Waterhouse, and I will carry on.

While I am lying in a hammock drinking coconut juice and the Isthmus sands blow through my hair, I'll be thinking and planning and praying for the Tojolabal people further south who are hidden away in the mountains. Wasn't it Samuel Rutherford who said, "He is no idle husbandman, He purposeth a crop." I can't be discouraged before Him, and you can't either. That is the secret—I am before Him. I want to stay before Him until I see the Tojolabal people delivered from the heavy burden of animistic superstition. You must want to, too. Let's furrow our hearts by prayer.

Your friend to the Tojolabals, *Julia*

More Indian Trails

April 22, 1948

"It's all the way you look at it," said the old maid as she kissed the cow.

And so I could write you all about the tall, graceful palms waving in the balmy tropical air. Or mention the thin slice of the silvery new moon that hung so helpfully in the night sky. Then, there was the Southern Cross out there beyond with the Scorpion trailing his long length halfway across the heavens. He seems to be trying to overtake the Cross, but he never does. Or I might talk about the big Pacific whose waves wipe clean the shores so faithfully twice a day. That's all very well *but*...

There are times when you hurt so badly in that stiff Indian saddle that you want the whole world to know about it! And so instead you tell folks that the tropical air can be so burning that you wish you had brought three canteens instead of one. Or that traveling by night makes you so sleepy you wish 100 times you could get off that mule and pile down to sleep, even if the malarial mosquitoes do attack in droves! That dear old Pacific can make you powerfully seasick when you're hot and thirsty and hungry. About that time, you're hoping to never have to see it again!

But something quite nice happened at the end of that 30-hour trail [by mule]. As the second night closed in around us, and we were drawing near our desired haven, the friendliest light began to twinkle on a hill. It was a lighthouse. At the foot of the lighthouse, the Indians told me was Salina Cruz, our much-looked-forward-to destination. I cannot tell you how much that light helped. I'm glad for lighthouses, aren't you?

And now it all seems so easy because I'm in Mexico City again. I even laugh at myself that, of course, you can take it. You'll take many trails again and mostly gladly—because at the end of the Indian trails are people who need to know the love of God.

Yours, for more Indian trails, *Julia.*

I Wish I Were an Indian

After her trip to Salina Cruz, Julia visited her colleagues Nadine and Ken Weathers, who worked among the Tzotzil people. The uniqueness of the Tojolabal highland area was its proximity to clusters of other ethnic peoples that included the Chamula, Tzeltal, Tzotzil, Chol and Zoque. These, plus about a dozen more ethnic minorities, are part of the Mayan linguistic family. Each group has its own distinctive native dress and mutually unintelligible spoken language. In her June letter, which began with "Hello, you wonderful people," Julia apologizes to her friends for her two months of silence since her last correspondence and explains that she has been acting as a surrogate mother to the Weathers' two children.

June 1948

That silent intermission between letters really wasn't a silence at all. I played the role of a harried housewife at the Weathers house and found out that you can keep rather busy with two babies to care for and washing to do and being responsible to prepare three meals a day.

All the while, Nadine translated and Ken published a primer. The only thing silent about the whole four weeks was my tribute to wives

and mothers who raised children in pioneer
places and still had time for translation work. At
the end of that time, we said a hearty "praise the
Lord" for the compilation of the translation of
First John in Tzotzil.

Julia's first co-worker in her work among the Tojolabal
was Celia Douglas. It's not clear from the available evidence
how long they worked together before Celia left to get
married. The first mention of Francis Jackson, who became
Julia's long-time colleague, appears incidentally in
newsletters from 1951. In the meantime, Julia had a series
of temporary co-workers, one of whom was Betty Miller
from Canada. Julia introduced her as follows:

> Here are some points on Betty Miller, the other
> part, of "we."
>
> > New recruit from Canada.
> > Africa bound
> > Red haired, but definitely
> > Enjoys life
> > Assigned my temporary co-worker.
> > Plays accordion
> > Loves Indians.
> > You'd love her, too.

Then, in a clever soliloquy, with just a touch of irony in
which she imagines herself as a Tojolabal Indian, Julia
writes:

> Sometimes I wish I were an Indian. For instance,
> right now if I were, I'd just stick a few things in

my little woven shoulder bag and hike off for the village. But as the situation is, I, being a civilized American, wrestle with several suitcases and five boxes of groceries and two bags of fresh food and a typewriter and a bedroll and bargain for mules and a guide. Then I have to go to all the trouble of being happy even when the guide shows up several hours later than he said he would. Not to mention, of course, that I don't exactly enjoy lumbering along for eight or nine hours behind the long ears of a mule. That's why sometimes I wish I were an Indian.

But most of all I'm most glad to be who I am because, being who I am, I get to translate God's Word for people who've never had it. I know you'll be remembering this, too, because you know I can't do it alone. I need the constant help of Another.

One of His secretaries, *Julia*

Thankful for Safety Pins

The big news of 1948 was the restoration of the biblical Jewish homeland and the establishment of the State of Israel on May 14. Harry Truman upset Thomas Dewey for the U.S. presidency and Great Britain established its National Health Service. Julia's big news was her new kitten and settling into a rough dirt-floor house in the village of Comitán. This sleepy village of cobblestone and dirt streets, bisected by the Pan-American Highway, was notable for

being the last town of any size before the Guatemalan
border. Comitán was also notable for being the largest of
four Tojolabal municipalities.

August 1948

Dear Whoever-You-Are,

If homey details are what you like, here they are.
We now own a little white kitten that entertains
the Indians with its various antics. They've never
seen one so full of life—a good advertisement to
Borden's Evaporated Milk. And it's fulfilling its
purpose of keeping the rats from taking over.
Traps are ineffective here.

Fresh corn season has come, and we're
indulging. That, with squash and fresh peaches,
keeps us from having to open so many of those
precious cans of things on reserve in the
cupboards. We do have cans of meat, too, but
manage to buy fresh pork now and then or a
chicken. The Mexican tortilla serves well as a
bread substitute, and they are delicious toasted
over our charcoal fire.

We have a dirt floor and lack a ceiling.[2] There
are plans underway to have the place floored and
ceiled before winter winds come again. It is
burdensome to wear four and five layers of

---

[2] A typical Tojolabal house is a one-room wattle and daub structure
approximately 7x4 meters with a high-pitched thatch roof. It's not clear
from the record if this was the kind of house Julia was living in.

clothes. The garden is coming along well in spite of its novice planters. That should help the fresh vegetables situation. About the time we planted the garden, we made a pretty stone walk from the back door to the front gate.

Those unromantic everyday jobs of cooking and keeping house and washing clothes and writing letters and weeding the garden we carry on very routinely here, too. This is all apart from the number one reason we came and the work that goes with it. Maybe that's why the mending basket is bulging, and we're so thankful to the inventor of safety pins.

Mundanely yours, *Julia*

A Recipe for Translation

The basic task a Bible translator with the Summer Institute of Linguistics (SIL, Wycliffe's partner organization) is to work in a non-literate ethnic culture, learn the people's language and then translate the New Testament into that language. This, along with teaching people how to read their own language, was juxtaposed with the prayer that the translated Word of God would work for good in the heart of those helping in the translation. Julia described this process with her characteristic whimsy.

The Holidays, 1948

Dear Some of You,

After a lengthy seven-hour day, six-day-a week period of translation, I now have a recipe for translation: Dump plenty of prayer, a chapter of Mark and an Indian helper into a bowl. Stir well. Add several dashes of good humor, fold in lots of patience. Do this daily for five weeks and you'll have a translation of the Gospel of Mark. Imperfect still, but it's joy unspeakable and full of glory! Translation time was climaxed by seeing our language helper come under some old-fashioned conviction and, finally, a decision for the Author of the Book he helped translate. Today, he continues witnessing. And so the Word spreads among the people you prayed for.

Seasonally Yours, *Julia*

2

Christmas in Mexico, 1951

In the world of letters, 1951 was notable for the release of the book *Letters and Papers from Prison* by the German theologian Dietrich Bonhoeffer. Bonhoeffer, who was martyred by the Nazis in April 1945, left a legacy both by his life and writing that was to be an ongoing challenge for the Western Church. Principally, the challenge was how to acknowledge God's enduring and comforting presence in the face of suffering at the hands of a godless world.

There was no direct correlation between Bonhoeffer's letters and those of Julia's, except that, in Julia's case, there was the expectation for people to be informed and the invitation to help share the load of her ministry among the Tojolabals. And because she knew the load was heavier than she could bear alone, she began what was to become her signature salutation:

"Dear Aaron and Hur."

The reference to Aaron and Hur would not be lost to readers of the Old Testament. In Exodus, the story tells how Moses, being too old to fight, appointed Joshua to do battle against the Amalekites and then positioned himself on a hill overlooking the battleground. There he held the rod of the Lord with uplifted arms. As long as Moses held up the rod, the Israelites prevailed. But when Moses grew tired and let down the rod, the Amakelites prevailed. At that point two faithful friends, Aaron and Hur, stood on each side of Moses and held up his arms. The Scripture says, *"So his hands held steady until sunset."* As a result, Joshua overwhelmed the army of the Amalekites in battle (Exodus 17:12-13).

In his book, *A Fresh look at Exodus,* Bernard Ramm explains that *"The rod of the Lord was the sign that it was God's strength and God's enablement that brought the victory. When the rod dropped it meant that Israel was fighting with her own strength and could not prevail."*[3] For the next thirty years, Julia began her newsletters with her signature salutation. She never wanted to let herself or her supporting partners and friends forget that to succeed in the spiritual battle, the Christian's strength and wisdom must come from God.

In a letter to "Dear Aaron and Hur" written from Comitán in January, 1951,[4] Julia begins with an admission

---

[3] Bernard L. Ramm, *His Way Out, A Fresh Look at Exodus* (Glendale California: G/L Publications, Regal Books, 1974), p. 106.

[4] Unhappily, not all of Julia's letters survived. There is a three-year gap from 1948 to 1951 with no personal record of her activities among the Tojolabals. As an archivist and historian, I am saddened by this loss of information concerning the early years of the Tojolabal church and translation program. However, the transition from 1948 to 1951 is not too jarring and the reader will hardly notice the gap.

that she is receiving letters from people she "can't recall." Yet, in spite of her lapse of memory, she is grateful for their letters and asks if they might refresh her memory and explain how it is they know her. She then describes how she and her co-worker celebrated Christmas:

> There was no [Christmas] tree or snow or icicles or poinsettias, in fact, you would have never suspected that Christmas was near. However, we did, because we're in the "know." We know that tissue paper flowers strung on strings drooped from the ceiling to all corners of the room, and palm branches with orchids between nailed along the walls and pine needles on the floor is Christmas, Christmas in Mexico! By seven-thirty, the little house by the side of the road was packed with Indians dressed in their finest garb. Even with the scarcity of gasoline, we had enough for two gasoline lanterns burning brightly. Everything looked lovely.
>
> Our singing wasn't professional, but we made a joyful noise to the Lord. The wee group of us Christians had practiced hard and faithfully with Serafin to accompany us on his guitar. We sang in Spanish and then Enrique and I sang in Tojolabal. Enrique was at his best. He wore Indian sandals instead of shoes. He had shoes, but he humbled himself. I was glad because we were celebrating the birthday of Someone else who had humbled Himself.

The flannelgraph lesson Enrique gave was
excellent. He sketched the life of our Lord,
ending with a triumphant note of His coming
again. For me, one of the biggest blessings was
watching the faces of the children as they
listened to the story. They were made happy
with gifts that cost us about five cents apiece.
Everyone was served coffee and cake. Results
have been gratifying with many asking about the
gospel who heretofore have been disinterested.
There is a good group of folks who are "almost
persuaded" but waiting for someone else to
move. Will you pray through that move?

Frances Jackson, who joined me as my
permanent co-worker, spent the holidays with
her family in the States. She is back with me, and
I am glad. We have some new members of the
family—a lovely little radio from a friend in the
US, and an old-fashioned hand sewing machine
that Frances picked up in the market in Mexico
City. We hope it won't turn into a white
elephant!

Your happy servant in Mexico, *Julia*

Julia's February two-page letter had two large hand
drawn maps. One was of Mexico and the other, the state of
Chiapas. The letter was Julia's attempt to help enlighten her
supporters with a few facts about Mexico and the area
where she worked among the Tojolabals.

Head Food

February 1951

Dear Aaron and Hur,

I know you've meant to dig out those maps to see "where that Julia Supple works" but you haven't had time. So here you are. By the way you have addressed me I've noticed you're utterly confused, and it's all my fault. First of all, Chiapas is a state, just like Pennsylvania or Oregon are states. The State of Chiapas borders on Central America. The topography is rugged with climates ranging from very hot and tropical to very cold in the high mountains. Not far are the nation's most unevangelized sections— Campeche and Quintana Roo. That is a jungle.

Forty hours of travel by bus and horseback from the house by the side of the road brings you to Mexico City. It is the Mecca of Mexico where all her sons dream of going someday. For us, it means a good hot bath and a real taste of civilization. It also means 24 hours of travel to the U.S. border city of Laredo.

Occasionally, I have written you from Mexico City. Our headquarters address there is Apartado 2975. That does not mean "apartment." It means "Box." Our street address is Heroes #53. Then there is the confusing "Mexico, D.F." which simply means Federal District, like Washington, D.C.

As I write this letter, I am still in Comitán, Chiapas. This is the town where we receive our mail. For years we've rented a room from a reliable family so that when we come in from the village, we have a place to stay and do our own cooking and where we keep our "town" clothes. Comitán has about 18,000 inhabitants with no single gospel witness.

From Comitán we take a local bus for about an hour and half over a terrible road to a little *pueblo* called Las Margaritas. Here we are welcomed into the homes of Christian believers. There is a well-established Presbyterian work here. From Las Margaritas we go by horseback to the place we love best, Jotana (Hoe-tan-nah). This is the village we've been talking about. This is home. That horseback trip is four hours long. We could go directly from Comitán to Jotana but it would be a long eight-hour horseback trip and we couldn't visit with the Christians. Jotana is the largest Indian settlement with some 700 inhabitants.

For the next two months we will be translating with Enrique in the town of Las Casas (see map). Fellow colleagues Ken and Nadine Weathers who live there are letting us use a vacant house of theirs. Las Casas is high in the mountains and very cold. Tuxtla, the state capital of Chiapas, is low, dry and hot. This letter is also dry. I'd rather write about something interesting. But this is "head food." Maybe next time it will be "heart food."

Matthew, the writer of the first New Testament Gospel, noted a reality that has been tragically true from the beginning of Jesus' ministry. Namely, that when people begin to believe the gospel message and seek to live their lives in conformity to the will of God, violent people begin a counterattack against them. Or, as the King James Bible translates Matthew 11:12, *"The Kingdom of heaven suffereth violence."* The first paragraph of Julia's May 1951 letter tells distressing news of what happened to a new believer.

The Kingdom of Heaven Suffers Violence

May 1951
Dear Aaron and Hur,

The other day in a village near here a man was stripped of his clothing, hung from the rafters by his arms and cruelly beaten. The reason? His love and devotion to Jesus Christ as Lord and Savior.

In Numbers 12:7, we are told that God can and will speak to people in dreams, as dozens of biblical characters have attested. This seems particularly true among people in Third World communities where often there is confusion among those who are hearing the gospel story for the first time. Following the story of the man who was beaten for his new-found faith in Christ, Julia continued with this story:

Victor is a near neighbor of ours who had a beautiful dream of the Lord who told him that what we teach is *the truth and to believe it.* Victor then told us that he does believe it. But he also adds that because of the attitude and complications with the town and tribal authorities, he might continue to have two allegiances, one openly to the village shrine, and one secretly to Jesus Christ. Our prayer request for Victor is for him to have the courage to openly confess the truth of his faith as his dream urged him to do.

Julia ended her May letter with the announcement that Wycliffe had asked her to do a summer speaking tour of the Eastern United States. However, before signing off she gave her readers this quiet gem:

Today, that boy for whom you have prayed follows on to know the Lord. After that we were able to check the gospel of Mark for publication and to finish a first draft of Acts. We were given courage to know that by many tribulations, we shall inherit the Kingdom of God. And we were made glad because He had come close to tell us.

After speaking every day at eight summer conferences, Julia ended the summer by attending Wycliffe's biennial conference, then held in Sulphur Springs, Arkansas.

Knee Work

October 3, 1951

Didn't our hearts burn within us when we heard [Uncle Cam Townsend and others of our leaders speak] that God has given us a greater vision for action in taking the gospel to the thousand tribal groups that can actually be reached in our lifetime?

Now for some news about the Tojolabals. There is much to tell you, but I shun long, detailed letters. However, I will mention that our relationship in the village where we work is, at the moment, precarious. Many would like to see us leave. A few have honored Christ and made Him feel at home. That is the trouble. He will always have enemies and so will we because we are His. Do talk to God about us, won't you? I intend to write you more often to keep you up to date. Another prayer list is enclosed for your knee work.

Expectantly His, *Julia*

From Comitán, Julia wrote two separate letters for the month of December. The first was full of homey details that included Frances canning eight pints of beef with the anticipation of adding pork to their list of stores. However, Julia had a problem with pork.

Critical Days

December 1951

Pork comes from pigs, and pigs on the hoof on the way to market can be terribly uncooperative and run lickety split when you least expect them to.

Now that I have your attention, let me tell you about Victor, the young man on your prayer list. He recently has come out for the Lord. His timidity and fear seem to have disappeared. But if there is any way of accurately measuring joys, I think my biggest one is Antonio.

He is fortyish and balding. Before we left the village last spring, he made his final decision for the Lord. Since then I have been constantly thrilled and amazed at the way the Spirit of God teaches these unlettered people. His explanation of the Godhead to another Indian man was better than most Bible School students could give.

Julia's second letter continued with the theme of joyfulness over the two "green blades," Antonio and Victor, who, having made their faith known, were summoned by an angry crowd of villagers who demanded to know why they had left the tradition of the elders and their tribal ways. Said Julia:

The experience of openly declaring their faith has made Antonio and Victor much stronger.

They are now excited with plans to take the victrola[5] and evangelize two neighboring villages. Every night we have a Bible study. And as in the book of Acts, "They gladly received the Word," and "daily in every house they cease not to teach and preach Jesus Christ."

When I mention Bible Study, I'm sure the picture in your mind is far from accurate. None but Enrique can read. It is really shockingly informal. Because the kitchen is the warmest room in the house, we usually gather there. Victor inevitably manages to find a paring knife with which he unconsciously strokes the back of his neck. One night He found a pencil and wrote his name on the wall. I've wanted to count the number of times the group spits on the floor during the evening. It takes all my mental faculties to concentrate on Tololabal and the lesson at hand. But the best of all is the divine touch on these Indians faces. Once they were blind, now they see! That is pure delight.

There is a rather large group for which I request earnest hard-stirring prayer—it is the Fearful-Almost-Persuaded group. They have heard the Word. They want to believe but fear to step out because of hostile relatives and friends. Will you

---

[5] Julia used the available technology of her day, including a hand-wound phonograph player and flannelgraphs. These would eventually give way to filmstrips, movies, cassettes, CDs, computers and the printed page.

bunch together and pray that the Holy Spirit shall burn the spirits of fear away?

Let me tell you about our Christmas program. Two very happy men, Victor and Antonio, gathered an armful of orchids and a bag of pine needles. We made bread and made cheerful decorations. Our home was too small for the crowd. The program was simple. We used a flannelgraph and larger picture rolls to illustrate. Some received it with gladness and others said it was of the devil. There is still much hatred against the Christ of God in dark places of this earth.

Julia ended her lengthy newsletter with an urgent SOS.

Here is an SOS for special prayer. Saturday evening, December 29, the villagers had a secret meeting in which it was decided to expel us from the village. On Sunday morning, the Christian men were called before the angry villagers. God gave special courage and wise answers, but the result was they, too, were ordered out of the village. Will you stand by us in these critical days?

Yours in His joy, *Julia*

3

The Fellowship of His Suffering, 1952

The deadline was set for January 6. That was the date given by the elders and most of the people in the village of Jotana for Julia, Frances and the small group of Christians to leave town. The ultimatum was that if they had not left by then, the villagers would forcibly enter the homes of the believers, including Julia's, and physically expel them and their belongings.

> From December 30 to January 5, we were under a great deal of tension. The villagers had threatened to enter all our homes and throw out our things. That was to have been on January 6th. There was nothing we could do but pray and commit the situation to the Lord. In the meantime, Enrique went to town to try to get someone with a sense of justice to enforce Mexico's perfectly splendid religious liberty law.

But that was not easy. In fact, he returned on Saturday with nothing concrete to help us.

But then on Saturday about noon our hopes soared when we heard the sound of a small airplane. We ran to the air field, and to our surprise, John McIntosh, one of our SIL directors from Mexico City, stepped out of the plane. A half-hour later the plane landed again, this time with a Mexican government official. John and the Mexican official met with the villagers on Sunday morning. That was a meeting I'll never forget. Francis and I stood before all the people while with one voice the villagers gave us the worst going over I ever had. They cursed and blasphemed in Tojolabal. Enrique and Anthony also stood before the madding crowd. Victor was at the airfield guarding the plane. As a result of that meeting, we were not run out of town. We hope that villagers understood there are higher authorities in place. But their anger is perhaps even more than before. We can only trust in God to bring glory out of all this. I know you'll pray for us all.

In the past, our kitchen was filled with eager listeners to the gospel. It has now dwindled to a faithful few. Valiant Anthony was literally sick at heart on Sunday night. He said he had never been so sad in all his life but never once did he think of recanting. You must remember this blast has come upon believers who are only two months old in the Lord. Would you pray that they may learn to hide in the Cleft of the Rock? Very few have been brave enough to venture to our home this week. When we walk outside, some of the people spit when they see us.

As I write, I am reminded that a few days ago, under our big avocado tree, I had an earnest conversation with my Friend. I wanted to know Him and the power of His resurrection and the fellowship of His sufferings.

The next month, after a ten-hour horseback ride from the village of Jotana to Comitán, Julia and Frances settled in to resupply their stores and catch up on their correspondence.

Don't Forget the Lepers

February 11, 1952

After spending two months in Jotana, we've come to Comitán to do our buying and more canning. Let me bring you up-to-date and share a series of lovely miracles that have happened. Following our last prayer letter, our village situation became even more serious than it had been. Ofracio, Victor's younger brother, was shot at. After that happened, we learned three men were being paid to kill all the believers. We despaired of help from the authorities because we had tried before to get help with no results. And again, the place of despair is a good place to be because it gives fiber to the waiting soul.

Then mysterious things began to happen. It was the outworking of you who fervently prayed during those difficult days. For about eight days we had no idea what was happening. We knew the village authorities were running back and forth to Las Margaritas and Comitán. At the end of that time, Lorenzo, the village president, called another town meeting and told them there was absolutely nothing they could do. He explained that under Mexican law, the believers are covered and any violence done to harm them would bring no end of trouble. Further, we learned the town authorities had to sign papers saying they would do the believers no harm. I relate these details to show there is a golden link in a beautiful chain of God's loving care for a couple of very undeserving women Bible translators and a little group of His believers.

There are no words to convey our heartfelt gratitude to you who have stood by us these anxious hours. My concern is that our Lord should receive, from our hearts and yours, just as much loving praise as He received concerned petition. Don't let us forget the ten lepers.

Thankfully His, *Julia*

Sometimes retreat is the better part of valor. At least Julia's next letter would indicate as much.

A Trip to Las Margaritas

March 13, 1952

Dear Aaron and Hur,

I am writing this from Las Margaritas. The reason, about twelve days ago a young man named Aurelio (it almost sounds like radio in English) showed up in the village and was eager to help us translate. For several days, we wrestled with Psalm twenty-three. I then suggested he pretend he was a little sheep. After that, the translation went much smoother.

Then one day the enemy of our souls got busy and whispered "evangelical" in the ears of a few of the villagers. In their minds, this word is a synonym for "devil" so it didn't take long for unrest to begin to stir. After all, you would object, too, if you thought the "devil" incarnated was living on your block!

So it seemed wise to avoid further trouble, and we packed a few necessary things, put them on a couple of horses and came to Las Margaritas. Now every weekday at 8:30, Aurelio and I sit down to translate. We keep at it all day until six, with two hours out for lunch and rest.

I dislike boring you with the same prayer

requests, but our village trouble still takes preeminence. The Lord knows just how hot to heat the furnace. During these days, comforts in many forms have pillowed us round about. In your letters, many of you have said just the right word I needed. Some have slipped in a tract with a similar word of encouragement. But please continue to pray. Ten days ago a group of angry men entered Victor's home to do him bodily harm. Fortunately, Victor suspected trouble and had hidden so nothing came of it. So please do not slacken on this request.

If you came to see us, we'd give you one of our three chairs to sit on. Our only other furniture are beds and tables. But we do have pictures cut out of Arizona Highways Scotched-taped on the walls to make the place look real homey.

Yours in His happy service, *Julia*

At the conclusion of her March 13th letter, Julia mentioned that she, along with Frances and eight Tojolabals, were making plans to spend Easter week with translator Marianna Slocum and nurse Florence Gerdel, an SIL team who worked among the Tzeltal people in the village of Corralito. Aware of the difficulty that Julia and Frances were experiencing among the Tojolabals, Marianna hoped they would be encouraged by the vibrant Tzeltal church. Earlier in her ministry among the Tzeltals, Marianna had experienced hostilities similar to those Julia was experiencing. Now, after eight years of patient prayerful translation ministry, there were over a thousand Tzeltal believers. Further, the Tzeltal Christian community was having an Acts 2:47 experience, "*And the Lord added to their number daily those who were being saved.*"[6] Unfortunately, just as Julia was about to leave, she received word that a serious measles epidemic had broken out among the Tzeltals in Corralito.

A Trip Deferred and Love Knows What to Do

April 19, 1952

At the last moment, we received word of a measles epidemic among [the Tzeltals] and all Easter programs have been cancelled. Under the circumstances, it seemed best to change our plans. Now we are glad we did since we learned of twenty deaths among them. For us here among the Tojolabals, Aureilio came to our house on Good Friday and told us his father said he could no longer testify in his home or in their village. Sunny Aurelio was cloudy that day. We committed this young man to the One who endured the contradictions of sinners. Aureilio is here in Las Casas (I write you from here) in the Bible Institute.

On Easter Sunday evening word leaked out there

---

[6] For more on the ministry among the Tzeltal, see Marianna Slocum with Grace Watkins, *The Good Seed,* (Orange, California: Promise Publishing Company, 1988).

would be refreshments, so a few extra people were there. We had several meetings during the week, but reviewed the story that evening. The whole story, of course, is so solemn and holy that our hearts prostrated before Him. We knew that mountain sides and deserts bare, torrent streams and battlefields were only a natural part of embracing His cross.

Julia added a P.S. to this letter indicating that she would spend several weeks at the SIL headquarters in Mexico City. She wanted to make a short Tojolabal dictionary, a hymnal, and, most importantly, ready the Gospel of Mark for publication. Living and working in the SIL cramped headquarters building on Heroes Street, number 53, was like living in a fish bowl. However, there were some redeeming features, one of which was the Sunday evening informal worship service.

The meetings usually centered around reports from those SIL workers who happened to be in the city. Most often members came to the city for medical reasons, or to renew their government papers, or, as in Julia's case, to work on their language materials. If they were there over a Sunday night, they were given an opportunity to report on what was happening among the people with whom they worked. Sometimes the reports sounded as if taken from the book of Acts. And while Julia hadn't been able to make the trip to see the Tzeltal church in Corralito, she did get to hear Marianna's report.

June 1952

Dear Aaron and Hur,

I wished a wish last night. I wished you could have been transported down here to breathe with me the exhilarating bracing winds that God's Spirit is blowing on the Tzeltal Indian people. It was a holy hour as a group of us gathered on Sunday night to hear reports of our SIL colleagues' work in their different allocations.

We heard how in two and half years, the Lord of the Harvest has gathered 2000 Tzeltals to Himself. We heard of the formation of an entirely indigenous-governed, indigenous-disciplined, and indigenous self-supporting church. It seemed we could almost hear their hearts raised in gladness of song and praise to Him who is always full of tenderness for the hurt things of life. He is seeking and finding His sheep on the mountains. He is coming down like rain on mown grass, as showers water the earth.

After the meeting on Sunday, my heart said one thing, "Nothing less, Lord, Nothing less." No lowering of standards. No rationalizing. No curtailing of God's power for the Tojolabals. Do Thou for me, O Lord. Do Thou for them.

Julia had planned to finish her proofreading by the end

of May, but, as often happens, such work takes longer than anticipated. In her same June letter, she wrote:

> This is the last day of May. I had happily imagined myself heading south about this time. But there is still work to be done here. Mark is on its way to completion. Then there are other things. Frances has written words of encouragement from the Tojolabals. Life is full of all sorts of small pleasures.
>
> My heart's desire for this work is to plough a deep furrow. There have been days when the air was heavy with smoke from the pit. Then a handful of blessing falls in the way. So there is always something to awaken a song. "The Lord shall cause His glorious voice to be heard." When our equilibrium is threatened, it's good to make music.
>
> Yours in His triumph, *Julia*

Like the letters of the Apostle Paul, Julia's letters were written to meet an immediate need. And like Paul's letters, Julia opened her heart and mind to her readers on behalf of the people she had grown to love and care about. At the same time, Julia's letters sometimes contained wistful plaints mixed with descriptions of the mundane aspects of her life and ministry. Her last two letters of 1952 challenged her readers to interpret the deep longings of her heart.

Prayer Is Not Water Spilled on the Ground.

July 1952

Dear Aaron and Hur,

I've been debating about writing you so soon after my June letter, but prayer is not water spilled on the ground. There is always danger of focusing the fierce light of hell upon names mentioned here and yet never to mention what the Lord is doing is to defraud him of glory. And so I keep these messages coming your way.

There have been some lovely comings and goings since my last letter. An extra-special friend of long standing, Lois Hall, is spending the summer with me. Her reactions to Mexico are delightful. I'm doing my best to give her a picture of the real Mexico. We hopped a second-class bus to see the pyramids. The markets with all their splash and bustle and bargaining is no end of excitement. We bought exquisite orchid corsages in Xochimilco for twelve cents. Later, the long trip to Chiapas' mountains swallows one up into lasting, eternal thoughts.

The meetings of the Christians in the village went on in my absence. Some reports were encouraging. Some were sticky. There is much to do for these folks if they are to be led into a burning, glowing life of love. He waits to show

Himself in ravishing fullness but that never just "happens." We must go on in spite of the birds. So keep on praying you who should be praying. When the needs are great, and no definite words can be found to offer them to the Lord, Miss Carmichael reminds us that God takes little upside-down prayers and puts them right-side up. Lois and I will go to the village next week. I do not need to tell you more.

Yours, because His, *Julia Supple*

An Ordinary Day

October 1952

Dear Aaron and Hur,

Frances [Jackson] is back, and life is picking-up where I left it last April when I went to Mexico City to get the printing done. You'd be really surprised to know how very ordinary the life of a Bible translator can be. Weeks pass, and no translation works gets done. Enrique, the only competent translation helper I've ever had, is away at the moment.

But to tell you about that ordinariness ... today we sold some ribbon and beads and needles. We bought some eggs, and sold some tin cans and had several medical cases. That all takes time. I had a long and valuable conversation about spiritual things with Hilaria. Yesterday, the fiber of Christian character was again tested. Anthony and Victor were called up before the men of the village and asked point blank if they believed in San Francisco, the patron saint of the village. They answered bravely and truthfully. This agitation was caused by a forced contribution towards buying liquor for the fiesta of San Francisco. Of course, the young men did not give. God placed them under the running water of constant danger so that spiritual slovenliness may be removed.

When Delfina's father died, I arrived at her home sometime after his death. Delfina, who had maintained a constant vigil for many weeks, simply ran into my arms and poured out her grief. The dear unpretentious little tribeswoman is rock-like in her fidelity and has a heart of great love.

In spite of loneliness, there is something most exhilarating about being free from formal services and programs and stripped down to realities. Yesterday, we had the story of the blind man. "Yes," they shook their heads, "we, too we're blind, but now we see." In moments like that, I feel I have recaptured that radiant wonder that first accompanies salvation.

Yours in the folds of His great love, *Julia*

4

Faith as Real as
Potatoes, 1953 – 54

The stories that captured world attention in 1953 and
1954 ranged from the molecule to the mountain.
Nineteen fifty-three was the year the world first heard the
phrase "Double Helix" and learned how DNA worked.
The world also learned the names of two intrepid
mountaineers, Edmund Hillary and Tenzing Norkey, the
first two men to set foot on the summit of Mount Everest.

In 1954, Roger Bannister, believing mental discipline to
be as crucial to athletic victory as physical prowess, did the
impossible and ran the first four-minute mile. That same
year, fans of the diminutive Bilbo Baggins could read the
further adventures of his nephew and heir, Frodo, thus
inaugurating the unlikely rise to celebrity of the Oxford
professor, J.R.R. Tolkien.

Wycliffe Bible Translators and SIL also had two notable
firsts. In 1953, the first Asia Branch of SIL opened in the
Philippines. And in 1954, the North American Branch of
SIL celebrated with Faith Hill and Faye Edgerton,

translators of the first published New Testament for the Navajo people of Arizona, New Mexico, Colorado and Utah. For Julia, 1953 was notable for an unexpected furlough. In her June letter, one of only three she wrote that year (or that remain in her collection), we learn that her mother, who lived alone, needed the assistance of her daughter.

Blessed To Be Among the Blessed

June 1953
Dear Aaron and Hur,

I've purposely delayed this letter. It has seemed wise to take a furlough a year earlier than planned [her first was in 1948]. Many of you know my mother lives alone [in Medford, Oregon] and cannot continue this way. Will you pray for us to know God's will every step of this dark wood, for we have not gone this way before?

I am busy setting things up for another to carry on in my absence. There are tag ends to gather up for a pedagogical grammar. New verb charts must be made and text translation to copy. In fact, there is enough to do that it sort of produces a paralysis, and I am most likely to sit down in the middle of it and just stare.

In an earlier letter Julia had, as she most often did, ended her letter with a challenge for "Aaron and Hur" to continue holding up the arms of the Lord's servant and for the Holy Spirit's intervention on behalf of the Tojolabals.

There are a number of props in God's Word, the kind of words upon which time and time again we've been caused to hope. One of these is: "And blessed is he, whosoever shall not be offended in Me." Sometimes the ways of prayer are baffling. You and I have stood in the gap for these tribespeople and yet the big thing we have asked for has failed to come. As yet, our "unconquerable Emmanuel has not ridden in the field on His white horse." It produces a sense of mystery, but "Blessed (how sweet that word!) is he, whosoever shall not be offended in Me."

Yours, to be among the blessed, *Julia*

One of the Mexico Branch's stated objectives was to foster a family spirit among its members. In many cases, the bonding that occurred through years of common experiences and trials endured together became as strong as blood ties. And nowhere in 1953 was that family spirit (with all of the common vicissitudes of a normal family) in evidence more than in the Mexico City headquarters. The building on Heroes Street 53 was affectionately known as "The Kettle." And like a true kettle, this once proud, handsome old sandstone hotel was always steaming with activity.

The Crossroad of a Million Private Lives

November 1953
Written in Mexico City
Dear Aaron and Hur,

I should like very much to describe the place we call the Kettle. In one of my last letters, I called it a fishbowl. However, someone else suggested it should be called "the crossroad of a million private lives." As we shuffle through its historic halls, it challenges all the mettle and vigor of fleeted youth, that same challenge that charges the adrenal glands at an August Clearance sale.

At every point someone is packing or unpacking, dealing with what to take [to the village] and what to leave, nailing a box or tying a bundle. Not to mention, of course, the dozen or two children whose happiness depends on screeching and screaming, and sliding or hopping. And through this veritable pandemonium comes the uncouth buzz of a power saw. It is veritable pandemonium with a door on it. In the midst of the aforesaid confusion, I am trying to have an elevated thought or two to make this letter worthwhile.

By 1953, it was evident that the Mexico branch of SIL needed larger and more efficient headquarters to accommodate and serve the growing number of new members being added year by year. Since the Heroes Street headquarters could not adequately accommodate all the Mexico members, the one true family reunion time came at the biennial conference held in Sulphur Springs, Arkansas.

> I just love Wycliffe conferences. They come every two years. In addition to the rich warm fellowship with our colleagues, some of whom we haven't seen since the previous conference, we have speakers and devotional times that charge us and fill us with purpose and plans of giving God's Word to all the ethnic groups in Mexico and beyond. We feel, as one person aptly said, "It's like we are handling live wires as we enter the mind and desire of the living God." What an exalted privilege!

In the midst of this exuberant letter, there was an "oh by the way" sentence that said simply her year's furlough plans had changed, her mother was doing much better and she had spent a month's vacation in Arizona.

> I had hoped to sit and soak in some spiritual atmosphere while vacationing. But somehow I slipped into a mad whirl of civilized life, managing to speak about twenty times. My blessing came in small bundles, however, and I crossed the Mexican border with enough spark to survive the rude interruption of having my new Zenith Transoceanic Radio confiscated.

This was another challenge to faith, and said Zenith will soon be happily trundling to Jotana by Indian back.

In a few days we'll be back where life takes on a certain pattern and tranquility because we get back to where we know God has planned for us to be among the Tojolabals. At least we aren't exhausted at day's end by pushing buttons and maneuvering gadgets. Instead we like that exhilarated exhaustion that accompanies a good bout of translation, or simply being hands and feet for the Lord Jesus.

Yours in Calvary bonds, *Julia*

Faith Seeking Understanding

To be sure, Julia was an explorer of ideas and spiritual insight. Her first letter of 1954 began as follows:

January 1954

I find myself now and then doing what may be fanciful thinking about celestial things.

Here was faith seeking understanding, and she admitted that such probing left her curiosity satisfied "with things of which we only get fleeting glances." Julia then interrupted her esoteric musings with a practical report about Christmas in the village.

Any outsider who may have dropped in on Christmas Eve would have supposed we had everyone in the village as friends. The house was packed. The eagerness to drink a cup of coffee and have a piece of cake belied the usual interference and often outright hostility so many have displayed. So we take advantage of the season and speak a word in season and pray that God will prepare good ground in some prepared heart.

Yours in New Year blessings, *Julia*

Out of the Mouth of Babes

February 1954

Dear Aaron and Hur,

One Sunday night in January the children in the village were awed to be handed a newly translated hymn book and asked to choose their favorite hymn to sing. Javier, the extrovert, got the ball rolling with his request. When we adults joined our voices with baby voices I thought, "Out of the mouth of babes and suckling Thou hast perfect praise." There must be no sweeter music in His ears than praise sung by little children.

Then with uncompromising candor, Julia proceeded to challenge her supporting partners with the reality of what it's like to work with a people who are indifferent, suspicious and often hostile enough to kill, and at the same time continue with the job of translation.

The intention of my letters are to solicit prayer. For that reason, I do not want to attempt to disguise facts or the concern this work or these people cause me. In some ways, the few believers are ahead of ordinary church goers at home. Without complaints, they receive the constant taunts of their companions. They seem sincere in their love for God. They are not mercenary. I was quite encouraged lately when Anthony asked if Christians shouldn't be cleaner than other people.

On the other hand, it's very difficult to have regular services. Other things easily interrupt them. As far as evangelization in this village, it appears at a standstill. Fear has gripped many, and no one comes out. There are villages all around us, and we have been prevented from going. I get tempted to depression, which is spiritual paralysis.

Meanwhile, I press on with translation. My goal is to get John and Acts revised enough for a trial edition by furlough time. This takes hours of my day and part of the evening for checking with Enrique. Frances is having some simple reading lesson with the children and Delfina. Now this is all fuel for prayer.

There are hundreds of snags in translation work. We've recently struggled with how to say, *"That which is born of the flesh is flesh."* We can't use the word for "meat" and if we refer to the flesh part of the human body, it must be possessed. So shall we say, "our flesh" or "his flesh" or should we take the dangerous liberty of interpretation and say, "That which is born of human beings is human beings"? And those amazing reading classes in the light of pine torches! And both translation and reading classes are kept lively by an ample supply of fleas and baby Nadine making the rounds to deliver her darling kisses. These are sidelights we won't include in the preface of the forthcoming books!

At this time of year, I'm reminded that

Age is a funny thing:
Cherished in a tree,
And cheese
And furniture
And wine—
Most everything
But me. (Helen K. Beacham.)

I thought you might like that. So many of us are in the same boat.

Agingly yours, *Julia*

March 1954
Written in Comitán (Ko-me-táhn)
Dear Aaron and Hur,

This town is the last of any size on the Pan-American Highway before you get to Guatemala.

Burros still lumber up and down its cobblestone streets delivering soda pop to the stores. To us this means fresh meat, fruit and vegetables, and madly rushing around to replenish our exhausted supplies. We maintain a rented room with a Mexican family.

We have been isolationists for almost three months. Subscription to Newsweek has expired, and the radio hasn't come. I was almost at the point of taking off my shoes and going completely native, when behold, dear Zenith came bouncing up to the door. After hungrily devouring six newscasts, we felt like powdering our noses, booing Molotov and acting civilized.

There have been three earnest inquiries into spiritual things during February. Each is a story in itself. Don Carlos, a big burly schoolteacher, hates everything in general and Americans, in particular. But the Holy Spirit worked and after listening to the gospel and my promising to pray for him, he kissed my hand. I don't know who was more surprised, he or I! Ruben is going from bad to worse; it is a fearful thing to fall into the hands of an angry God.

Julia

In 1955, the importance of doing linguistic surveys among the ethnic minority languages of Mexico was just beginning to be realized. L.L. Legters, the co-founder of

Wycliffe with Cameron Townsend, had, in the nineteen twenties and early thirties, pioneered linguistic surveys in Brazil, Mexico and Central America. Years later, under the leadership of men like Dave Persons, the theory and practice of linguistic surveys, and their link to Bible translation, would be developed into a fine art. One of the chief goals in doing a linguistic survey is to determine what constitutes a separate language as opposed to a dialect variation. This information is vital to determine whether a Bible translated for one group would be intelligible to a second group, where, for example, both groups share the same tribal name but are separated by a mountain range and thirty miles of ill-kept paths.

In April 1954, five months after her last letter, Julia informed her supporters that she (although not calling it a linguistic survey) wanted to visit another Tojolabal group some distance away. In an earlier letter, she wrote that lack of funds had made such a trip impossible. Then she said:

> One evening in February as we sat chatting around an Indian fire, Anthony expressed a desire to go with us and said, "Why should we wait another year?" Some roads are impassable except in March. Then came one of those golden moments when the Spirit meets spirit and assurance is given. Since then an ample supply of saddles are in the making. Horses will be arranged, and I have bought a saucy new straw hat to boost morale.

A Macedonian Call

April 1954

I suspect basically I'm afraid of people. But even worse, I have a horror of people being afraid of me. So when the Tojolabals of our village told me the mountain Tojolabals would be afraid of me, I almost chickened out and didn't want to go. But later, a way over in San Isidro when a little child ran his hand lovingly through my hair and said sweet nothings to me, I was glad I'd overcome my cowardice.

And it's San Isidro that I would like to tell you about. It was here we discovered not every Tojolabal has a heart of steel. The people of San Isidro received us with open arms. They were amazed that two white women could speak their very own language. As such they listened eagerly and devoured the gospel message on the portable victrola. Every person in town must have been there. Since we told the story simply and adequately, we decided against their invitation to stay. Then three representatives from the town of Las Cruces came and begged us to come to their town. When we arrived, every man had stayed home from work to listen to the message on the victrola. They gave us food and beds. Surely this was a Macedonian call.

The records were played over and over. Then our own Victor in his humble Indian way told the crowd what God had done for him. What followed were many intelligent questions and what appeared to be earnest inquiry. We talked about the cost of taking our cross and following Jesus and how Jesus is calling mountain men to accept the challenge and ring the message far and wide.

As I lay that night on my plank bed, I could hear animated conversation from the nearby houses. Their talk was all about our Lord paying for their sins. Sadly, we left them the following day. Will you take the people from San Isidro on your hearts? The light has penetrated. Pray for the full burst of a new day.

The country we traversed was rich and green, a lavish jungle. As we returned to our village, we found parched earth. It is a dry year. Brave young corn are bowing their heads and dying. Eleven years with little fruit—a dry and thirsty land. Could it be that in our jungle country, God will call forth a crop? As Peter Marshall said, "We need a faith that is as real as fire, and prayer as real as potatoes."

Yours in His endurance, *Julia*

Almost without exception, those who participate in a language or linguistic survey experience some kind of unexpected calamity. This usually includes being stranded because of transportation breakdown, running out of food, getting lost, or just plain trail-weary fatigue.[7] In Julia's case:

> A train of ants marched into my mummy sleeping bag. Then there were ticks, and chiggers and such that one can only share with one's mother.

Group Service

Some people did it willingly. Others, when asked by the SIL Mexico branch to do their share of "group service," grumbled and wished those two words could be expunged from the English lexicon. In all fairness, such people were generally highly motivated to continue working on their translation program and were loath to leave the village to set up housekeeping in Mexico City. But, like a modern army, for every person in the field, there are at least five people behind the lines in supporting services. In addition to the work of buyers, secretaries, printers, people in publishing and finance and, of course, the director and his staff, there were those tapped for their public relations and speaking abilities. Julia was one of these. She had a proven track record as one who could tell the Wycliffe story with imagination and clarity and a challenge to Christian young people.

---

[7] As an example, pioneer missionary to Chiapas, John Kempers of the Reformed Church in America, reported on his survey trip that: "We slept in awful places, waded swollen rivers, crossed mountains, and muddy trails where the horses sunk up to their knees in mud, and I nearly died from food poisoning."

When Julia and Frances returned to Jotana after their survey trip to the mountain Tojolabals, it was their intention to remain in the village and continue working on translation. Then an MAF airplane dropped them a letter.

Under Divine Orders

July 1954

Dear Aaron and Hur,

You can't possibly be more surprised than I to tell you my mailing address has changed from Comitán, Mexico to Chicago. What a surprise. And yet the Christian life pledges us to be loyal followers of Captain Great who, as someone says, has no dull ideas at all, but only dynamically creative ones. And from the same Author I quote, "He delights in taking the most unlikely and most unsuitable material, such as the weak and foolish things of this world, and things, which ordinarily are despised, and using them in His campaigns to forward His designs in a way, which must be overwhelming, humiliating and infuriating to the Powers of Darkness."

On June 28th that delightful angel of the air, the Missionary Aviation Fellowship (MAF) plane, came swooping over our little village and dropped a letter for us. The great enemy of our souls arranged that the little landing strip should never be used again. Indians have planted cornfields there, which have never prospered. As per instructions from the Mexico Director, we hastily left the village [on horseback]. My instructions were to immediately replace someone on official deputation. Francis was to meet another SIL colleague in Tuxtla and be her temporary coworker. Thus, in the course of a few minutes, our best-laid plans were changed. We had thought the very reverse, that Frances was to have gone on furlough this fall and I not until next summer.

Julia gave the dates and places she was scheduled to speak in nine different locations from July 18 to September 6. She then ended her letter with words that were amazingly similar to those of martyred missionary Jim Eillot: *"He is no fool who gives what he cannot keep, to gain what he cannot lose."*[8]

It is no trivial affair to transmit God's creative, redemptive, saving thoughts to the minds of

---

[8] Jim Elliot, with four fellow missionaries, was martyred in Ecuador by Waodani (Auca) spears on January 8, 1956. In a journal entry dated October 28, 1949, Jim wrote: "He is no fool who gives what he cannot keep to gain that which he cannot lose." It is possible that both Jim and Julia heard a similar saying independently of each other. According to the Billy Graham Center Archives at Wheaton College in Illinois, "Philip Henry (1631-1696), father of well known preacher and Bible commentator Matthew Henry (1662-1714), was credited with a very similar saying. In *The Miscellaneous Works of the Rev. Matthew Henry…*, published in 1833, is a biography of Philip by Matthew. (The original biography had apparently been published in 1699.) On page 35 of the volume, Matthew is recalling his father's acts of kindness and charity and how he used to say, 'He is no fool who parts with what he cannot keep, when he is sure to be recompensed with what he cannot lose.'"

other people. It is a grave responsibility. It could mean life or death to thousands upon thousands of souls, for I go to find dedicated young men and women whose love for Him is expressed in obedience to His last command. Will you pray that the Lord of the Harvest will call forth laborers, God's chosen people, to beam the light to more of earth's dark recesses?

Yours, under divine orders, *Julia*

5

Stateside, 1955 – 57

The years 1956 through 1959 were some of most dramatic and far reaching in Wycliffe's early history. They were, in fact, important bridge years between the first "pioneering" phase of the organization and its later development. In 1956, Wycliffe's membership stood at five hundred. Three years later, the membership had more than doubled to over a thousand. Some of those new members joined the new work in Papua New Guinea that began in 1956, the first branch in the Pacific.

As for Julia, she would spend the next two and a half years looking after her mother, attending a business college and working a nine-to-five job. In her March 11, 1955 newsletter, one of only two from 1955 that remain in the archives, she told how her mother's house in Medford, Oregon was sold and of her move to Portland.

His Softest Whisper

March 11, 1955

This past January I enrolled in a fine business college here in Portland. With all the new

57

arrangements I have had to make, there have
been lovely evidences of His leading.
Apartments here, as everywhere, are high. Bus
fare in Portland is now twenty cents, so I felt
that if I could be downtown, it would save that
expense. Thus, I began tramping the streets for
apartments. The first day it seemed impossible to
find anything within my means, and the little
dank, dark lurks they unashamedly showed me
were unsuitable for my mother. The next day I
fairly prayed myself along the streets and looked
at more of the same variety. Almost despairing
of anything clean and decent for living, I saw a
sign and went to inquire. It was just what I
wanted—modest, clean with ample space. I had
asked the Lord for a private bath, good heat, and
two beds, with proximity to town. This was it.
But the price was too high for my budget. So
using the skills of my acquired Mexican
bargaining culture, I bargained with the landlord,
and he lowered the rent.

Shortly after I arrived in Oregon, my mother had
a grievous time of sickness. She suffers from
high blood pressure and related complications.
Recently she had a bad fall and her arthritis
flared up. With all this, I realized I would be tied
down and felt it well to be studying. I have
refreshed my business subjects for two reasons.
One, in case I should have to take a leave of
absence to stay longer with mother. If that

should happen, I would need to "make tents." And two, when I return to Mexico, it will be useful to me in my group service in the headquarter offices.

Julia's last paragraph informed her supporters that she was attending Central Bible Church, a short three blocks from her new apartment, and that she was enjoying sweet fellowship with new friends at the church. When they asked after her plans, she explained she had none except to look after her mother. She then wrote:

> My furlough is not actually finished until September 15. By that time He will have issued orders. You, of course, desire only God's will for me, and I ask you to pray that I shall not miss His softest whisper. Thank you!

Is There no End to His Comforts?

September 5, 1955

A good antidote to a "feeling low" mood is to sing the happiest songs one knows. I'm doing that today. The reason? My missionary colleagues are all together in Sulphur Springs, Arkansas. They are praying and rejoicing, plotting and planning new strategies and advancement into new fields of Bible translation opportunity. I cannot deny these days are difficult, and I would dearly love to be there.

However, for the present, my Commander has issued orders for me to be here with my mother who can no longer live alone. But with it all have come strong words of consolation that I devoured greedily. "The love of duty is the strength of heroes and there is no other way in life in which to learn that love." And so long ago, Henri Didon[9] said, "I do not want people who come to me under certain reservations. In battle you need soldiers who fear nothing (not even changed orders!)." Again, "Obedience leads to unexpected places and knows no precedents."

This leads me to tell you that I've had to rejoin the ranks of wage earners. My "sacred secularity" is a legal office with files, desks, typewriters and a small office force of those whose lives are ego-centric. One day when I was dwelling on these mundane thoughts, chafed in spirit, the Lord Himself drew quite near and gave me this:

> My potter's busy wheel is where
> I see a desk and office chair,
> and well I know the Lord is there.
> And all my work is for a King
> Who gives His potter songs to sing,
> Contented songs, through everything.
> And nothing is too small to tell
> To Him with whom His potters dwell
> My Counselor, Emmanuel.
> Master, Thy choice is good to me,

---

[9] Didon (1840-1900) was a Dominican preacher, writer and educator from Le Touvet, France.

It is a happy thing to be,
Here in my office—here with Thee.

Is there no end to His comforts?

Julia

For the next fifteen months there is a news blackout. Julia's next letter is a 1956 Christmas card.

A Joy Letter

The Holidays, 1956
Dear Aaron and Hur,

This is a joy letter. And surely that delightful substance is fitting for this season when true worshipers of God are meditating on the holy extravagance of Divine love to come in human flesh.

But sermonizing is not the purpose of this note. Rather it is to tell you I'm packing to head southward again. Some day when my bones are brittle and I must succumb to the inevitable sunset side of life, I purpose to record and fill in details that must be left unexplained for the present.

Suffice it to say that for months there has been a gradual unfolding of His purposes climaxing with the sudden and unexpected coming of my sister and her husband to be near mother. Following that, as if to confirm His Word, "This is the way, walk ye in it," I received a gift, large

enough, and from a surprising source, to relieve
any doubt as to His desire. Do you, too, wonder
at the purport of divine generosity?

Julia outlined her travel plans, which were to leave in
January or early February in the company of another
Wycliffe colleague. She then reminded her supporters that
to reach the village of Jotana would require a two-day bus
trip to the market town of Comitán and then another
twenty-eight miles by bus and horseback before she would
be reunited with the Tojolabals. But she admitted that
leaving home would be painful.

My joyous anticipated meeting with the
Tojolabals entails reluctant goodbyes with others
we love. Mothers of us missionaries love much
and consequently, suffer much. Need I say
more? But our great God mingles with a wholly
surrendered life and plants His impress upon it. I
have not dared to settle for anything less.

Joyously yours, *Julia*

In *Walden*, Henry David Thoreau wrote: "*I went to the
woods because I wished to live deliberately, to front only the essential
facts of life, and see if I could not learn what it had to teach.*" In
April 1956, Julia informs her supporters that she had, in
fact, been traveling deliberately not for the ephemeral
things of life, but for the essential things in her life, namely,
her ministry as a Bible translator among the Tojolabals of
Chiapas. Julia's April letter is notable for its decided

emotional current generated by being with new Wycliffe members who were full of idealism and promise.

Two of these new members were the tall and lean Blood brothers, David and Hank (Henry) from Portland, Oregon. It was in the Blood's car, driven by Mrs. Blood (David and Hank's mother), that Julia had spent six weeks traveling back to Mexico.

April 12, 1956

Two of the four passengers were a couple of fellows who almost didn't stop growing, six feet three-ers with a heart's desire to get going for God.[10] During the six weeks of travel, sometimes in the Bloods' car (Mrs. Blood drove the car and gave us Joshua 1:8 as our journeying verse), some on second class bus, a dugout canoe, horses and a missionary plane, we traveled the length of Mexico and all the way to my field of assignment. It's impossible to put into words the emotion I experienced in getting back to the field. I felt I would burst with happiness the night we arrived in Comitán.

After an absence of two and a half years, Julia's reentry among the Tojolabals came with some unexpected surprises. First was the language.

---

[10] David and Hank would be assigned to work in Vietnam. In 1968, Hank died while in the custody of the People's Liberation Armed Forces (the Viet Cong). See James and Marti Hefley, *No Time for Tombstones, Life and Death in the Vietnamese Jungle* (Wheaton, Illinois: Tyndale House Publishers, 1974).

October 1, 1957

After the first several days, I discovered I not only understand everything, but I am also able to express myself as well.

Julia's other surprise had to do with the poverty and rustic living conditions of the people and their common lack and use of soap. This, she said, stood in contrast to those whose lives had been transformed by the grace of God.

I am greatly encouraged to see how the Christians have grown in grace and their love to Christ. Even their outward appearance is a testimony to what has happened in their hearts.

In Jeremiah 30:2 the prophet writes: *"Write in a book for yourself all the words that I have spoken to you for human memory might forget them."* Many Christians have taken this passage as an admonition to journal. Julia's letters were in many ways a form of journaling and she often included even the mundane events of her life. In her July 11 letter, she wrote mostly about the problems of overseeing the renovation of her Portland apartment from a distance. But then in the midst of the mundane she offered this surprising paragraph:

I have never mentioned this before, but my co-worker, Frances Jackson, is an outstanding cook. When this fact became known to the directors at Jungle Camp, they asked if she could be reassigned to be the chief cook at Jungle Camp.[11] Frances had hoped a new assignment like this might never happen. But it did, and she loves the new challenge. In the meantime, my replacement co-worker is Peggy (Margaret) Wendell. Peggy has many gifts. She taught swimming at Jungle Camp, kept the camp's books and is herself a literacy expert. And with all of this she's warmhearted and full of good humor.

As a linguist and Bible translator, Julia's task was to work hard at uncovering and understanding the linguistic components of the Tojolabal's language. This was a necessary condition for producing a clear, grammatically correct and meaningful translation of the Scriptures. But Julia was more than just a linguistic technician, she was also an engaged, empathetic, sensitive participant in daily village life. But sometimes this involvement became perilous and highly emotional. This from her October letter:

> There is a strong enemy nucleus in our village. Their greatest strength is the venom of their

---

[11] Jungle Camp referred to a phase of training for new and potential SIL members. The Camp's pioneer setting (then held in the jungles of Southern Mexico) allowed for the testing and screening of applicants and the imparting of practical skills in preparation for the rigors of living and working in primitive conditions. The training also included physical, psychological and spiritual conditioning. As world conditions changed, Jungle Camp was discontinued in the 1970s and evolved into new methods of training for living and working among ethnic minority groups.

tongues, especially effective in town meetings. However, they not only speak, they act. The most recent was to fell a huge tree that completely blocked the entrance to the airfield two days before the plane was due to land. But we are not deceived, and we make our prayer unto our God and set a watch against them day and night. Our God shall fight for us.

These past months have been a time of crises for many of the Christian young people, and they have been willing to suffer for their faith. Alejandra is one of them. She is a beautiful tender-natured girl who will accompany us to a linguistic workshop in February. The caveat is that if she wholly follows her Lord, she may never be able to return to her home. Her father has decided to marry her to an unworthy man.

A lot of preparations are needed as we attend the linguistic workshop. Thus, we are planning to move temporarily to a nearby Spanish-speaking town and bury ourselves in linguistic data. Delfina and her two young sons will go with us. In those three small Tojolabals is all the information we will need. Just pray for us to discover it, to hear correctly, record it on file, and get those file slips in their proper slots. This must be done before the New Testament can speak Tojolabal, the Tojolabal way.

The New Testament is extraordinarily realistic about human troubles. There is no promise in Scripture that this life will be easy or painless or free from suffering. As Christians, we are told to expect trials, temptations and afflictions. In a world that is far from rational or fair, Paul wrote to Timothy to endure hardness like a good soldier (2 Timothy 2:3).

This was the world that Julia and her Wycliffe colleagues were called to serve and for which they were offered no explanations. Rather, they were (and are) simply called to act.

Our Gibraltar

In November, the juxtaposition of human need, linguistic classification and cultural anthropology came together in the person of Anthony. In her letter, Julia described how Anthony, suffering from a series of health problems, interpreted his first X-Ray procedure.

November 26, 1957

Dear Aaron and Hur,

Anthony is a star. He is one hundred percent Tojolabal in thought and speech and only under great pressure will he exude a word of Spanish. Since his stand for Christ five years ago, he has been our Gibraltar, enduring sharp criticisms and mocking from his peers, but continuing on strong in his faith.

However, preparing Anthony for an operation and an injection is another thing. Our patience has been stretched thin. At times, I felt my smile had nothing behind it but teeth. But we believe in happy endings, and we are readying ourselves to see him through a gallstone operation.

Down through corridors of time, no Tojolabal has ever had the experience of having his insides exposed to a picture-taking machine. After the X-ray, the diagnosis was an abscess on the liver and a number of gall stones in the biliary tract.

It sounded very professional to us, but when the diagnosis made the rounds of the village, we heard poor Anthony's liver was rotting, and he had a big rock in his stomach. And during all this, Tojolabal phonemes are flying around like sputniks. Catching them in their native habitat to record on 3 x 5's is fast making our files pudgy. And, incidentally, language files are nice when they're pudgy.

Thanksgivingly yours, *Julia*

Christmas Night, 1957

Julia and Peggy were both limp and exhausted after the equivalent of being a ringmaster to a Sunday School Christmas pageant. With feelings of "I'm glad it's over," they relaxed around a charcoal brazier.

Dear Aaron and Hur,

Poor little ragamuffins, each with a native bag slung from their heads, started out on the fifteen miles to their village. Papa Victor was to meet them halfway to help six-year-old Ester the rest of the way. Tonight they're sound asleep with happy dreams of the merriest of Christmases.

For several days our home has housed the dearest of children, each doing their part to make the Christmas celebration a successful one. We translated a jolly-worded rhyme to the tune of Jingle Bells which, with their arms around each other, they did in a masterful performance for the church program. They memorized Matthew's account of the Christmas story. One person sang Silent Night in Tojolabal. We thought they were at their best.

The program was the climax, but surrounding the climax was a whole series of small crises like, two baths in a period of only four days. With buckets of water and soap, we let cleanliness have its perfect work and five Tojolabal children simply shone. Then, there was the making of some two hundred tamales and stacks of cakes and pots of coffee. And the satisfying sharing of the good things with poorer neighbors. Is there anything dearer than an excited happy child? The Lover of Children drew near and granted us our portion of peace on earth and good will toward men.

Antonio was the main subject of our November letter, remember? By the good hand of God upon him, he is much healthier; he even made the fifteen-mile trip to Jotana to prove his liver hasn't rotted, and that he really doesn't have a rock in his stomach. But the gallstones are still with him, and complete healing, as we have asked, has not been granted. Operations of this kind are not done in Comitán, so on December 30, Antonia and his son Ricardo will leave for the Baptist hospital in the city of Puebla.

We ask for your prayers for this venture. Traveling with two ethnic people presents its own unique problems, like food and shelter. The comparison is like that of traveling with two people of color in the south. And also these two people have never ventured further away than the sleepy town of Comitán.

We have heard of a group of young people in Jotana who are turning toward the Light. Among them are Delfina's Golo who, you remember, came to Jesus' feet but under threatening, turned back. Prayer is *not* water spilled on the ground. His purposes are towards that village.

Expectantly your, *Julia*

In January, the month for looking both forward and backward, Julia shared some of the pain and "torrent of rough water" that she and Peggy had been going through, and then she gave an update on Antonio.

Puebla, Puebla

January 25, 1958

The operation on January 23 was a long and difficult one. The doctors gave us permission to be in the operating room where we stayed for the entire time. Even son Ricardo stayed for two of the four hours. I left the room with a deep and sincere appreciation of God's great gift to mankind, the medical surgeon. After that it was an eleven-hour vigil. I have not seen one flicker of a smile from Antonio. It seems that instead those strong words of Psalm 23 are more fitting. "Though I walk through the valley of the shadow of death I will fear no evil for thou art with me." Early this afternoon following those twenty-eight hours, he drifted nearer the shores of normality and at last caught a bit of sleep so that by 6:30 tonight he was asking for one of God's songs. And it warmed our hearts to know that our good friend Antonio will be given back to us.

It was a great relief and thankfulness to get to Puebla and by a series of circumstances to have every single need provided. Peggy and I have a small apartment a block from the hospital. The same doctor who gave Antonio an appointment on New Year's Day, also provided a bed and meals gratis for Ricardo in his daddy's room. Someone must have let the kind doctor know the best medicine an Indian can have is someone near who speaks his language and cares. There have been so many small "showings" that we are mighty suspicious Who that Someone is. "These are the edges of His ways" (Job 26:14). What will the full revelation be?

But lest Julia become too complacent, she related how Antonio, wanting to go for a walk on a cold day in his bare feet and being hindered by the nurses, sat down in the middle of the hospital lobby and refused to move.

On Monday, Ricardo came running for help. He was so tearful I didn't ask any questions. When I burst into the hospital lobby, I was, shall I say, startled to find Antonio sitting on the tile floor with five nurses and one doctor trying to persuade him to end his sit-down strike. When he wanted to go for a walk (the day was cold and windy), the heretofore helpful nurses refused to let him out. Thus, his only recourse was to sit right down where he was and pick the dead skin off his bare feet. When I agreed that he should go home, and that I'd go immediately and buy his bus ticket, only then did he go back to bed. However, the next day was warm and sunny, and he refused to budge out of bed. That is called "pulling an Anthony."

To live above with Saints we love.
Oh, that will be grace and glory!

To live below with Saints we know.
Well, that's another story!

Yours in the School of Patience, *Julia*

In her February 23 letter written from Las Margaritas, Julia told how, when Antonio was released from the hospital, they took a short walk through a beautiful nearby park. Antonio repeatedly remarked how perfectly God had made the world, and he continued to thank God for the miracle of his operation. Yet there was another miracle awaiting Antonio and one that he would never forget. Before Antonio and Ricardo made the long trip back to his village, they took a detour to Mexico City. Julia wanted Antonio and Ricardo to have the once-in-a-lifetime experience of attending the first ever Billy Graham preaching rally in Mexico.

When Antonio and his son climbed to the second gallery of the huge auditorium (he without difficulty) and saw eighteen thousand people and heard them singing some of the "God songs" Julia had translated into Tojolabal, Antonio was overcome. Heretofore, he was the persecuted minority in his village. In a real sense, he believed that he and the handful of believers in Jotana were the only evangelical Christians in the world. Now here before him were more people than he had ever seen in his life all gathered in one huge auditorium, believers in Jesus Christ singing His praises and listening to God's Word being preached from the same book Julia was translating into Tojolabal. In Julia's words, "When Antonio heard eighteen thousand voices blend to sing 'There is Power in the Blood,' his heart soared heaven-ward."

Join Wycliffe and See the World

As glorious as this experience was, one can only stay in the "heavenlies" for so long. The realities of life have a tendency to intrude. In this same letter, Julia shared what it was like to travel back to Las Margaritas by bus.

> Our trip home was not without incident. To provide more rest for the man minus a kidney, we tried it by stages. This involved moving about fifteen pieces of baggage and four people half a dozen times. How can some people look so crisp and chic when they travel? Not I. First, one of the party must jump off the bus, and then begin Operation Stuff, stuffing the stuff out of the windows and dragging the voluminous stuff off the racks, and finally off the bus in a sad, bedraggled state. After hunting for a hotel for us and then one for the Tojolabals, hiring two taxis to transport these "pilgrims" and their mountains of this world's goods, we finally fell exhausted into bed to regain strength for the same operation the next day. Do you want romance? Travel opportunity? Join Wycliffe and see the world!

> Food presents its problems. We finished a basketful on the trip, replenishing it occasionally,

but still we arrived with two starving men. Finding a fiesta and no hotel rooms in Comitán, we bedded down in a parked bus. That is, the rest of us bedded down. To stall off starvation, Antonio sat in the back chomping down some toasted tortillas. Happily, the young chap who slept on the bus to protect it was in a hilarious mood. We had a grand welcome at midnight and went right on to Las Margaritas on the same bus the following morning.

Many of you are keenly aware that the last three months have been months of strain and responsibility for Peggy and me. But I want to end this letter with great praise to God and profound thankfulness to all who have stood by [us in prayer]. With the help of modern medicines, Antonio's chances are good for a complete recovery from tuberculosis. Our hearts are singing for joy that we were allowed a part in his fight back to health.

Rejoicing Yours, *Julia*

6

The Rainy Season, 1958

The rainy season in southern Mexico brings lush greenery, clean air and cooler temperatures. It also brings rising rivers that isolate communities, and the once hard-packed dirt roads become impassable quagmires that impede the flow of people and cargo in and out of rural communities. Even bush pilots have difficulty with low-ceiling cloud cover.

The rainy season is also a wake-up call for those who procrastinated repairing their roofs, thatched or otherwise. With the first tropical deluge, such a house can become a leaking sieve. The last paragraph of Julia's February 23-March 3, 1958 letter made a passing reference to the coming rainy season three months hence and the inadequacy of their house against the expected seasonal rains. Julia also noted that space for their growing family was becoming a problem. However, in April, 1958, rain became a secondary cause for her concern.

In spite of the Mexican government's official position of freedom of religion and the desire for all its citizens, ethnic minorities included, to live in harmony and peace with one another, there was growing animosity against the fledgling group of Tojolabal Christian believers in Jotana. The hatred of evangelical Christians that began in the fifties would intensify over the next forty years. Persecutions would take several forms that included harassment, forced expulsion from their homes and lands, beating, false imprisonment and even killing.

It Never Rains but it Pours

April 26, 1958
Dear Aaron and Hur,

We are now plunging into a new and frightening experience for us. In three months the rainy season will be upon us, and our present housing is inadequate. We are presently a family of six with the potential to increase at any time. Delfina (one of our current family members) met a man in the village the other day that poured out his tale of woe about his daughter who might need protection for a time, say two or three months! Why, yes, she assured him. We'd be glad to take her in!

On Good Friday evening, the rumors of brewing evil alerted the Christian women and their children to take refuge in our house. We advised Antonio to come as well. But Antonio is Antonio, and he thought it unmanly and chose to stay alone in his house. Little did we know as the children, Esther, Lola, Peggy and I slept soundly, that Antonio was being stalked for the kill. Two men were waiting in his yard and would have killed him had he opened his door. Early Saturday morning, the two men left. Antonio escaped and hid in the hills. Then late on Saturday night the day when drinking and fighting among the Tojolabal men are at its worst, we heard a knock on our door. When we opened it, there stood a badly frightened Antonio. That's when we learned his story. Then, shortly after that we heard another knock on the door. Peggy shoved all the Christians into our bedroom and shut the door. When we opened it, there stood Pancho! He had freed himself from the group of drunks and risking his life, had come to see if Antonio was safe. So right there in our house were the most-wanted people in the village! Together we decided that Peggy and Pancho and Jeno, Delfina's youngest, should go to town and notify the police of our predicament. At 4:00 a.m. on Easter morning they set out.

It's not clear from her correspondence who sent the message to warn Julia and the others that they were in real danger. Thus, after seeing a spy in her back yard, Julia felt the sensible thing to do was to leave Jotana for the town of Las Margaritas.

We tried to get help to carry the babies. We had five children less than three years of age and only two Tojolabal women to carry them. When we asked for help, no one was willing to risk their lives. By 11:00 a.m. with only the clothes on our backs, we set out for Las Margaritas fifteen miles away. The most difficult thing, of course, was to leave before the eyes of all those who had mocked and persecuted the believers.

On the way out of the village, thirteen-year-old Christina saw us and grabbed up a baby, slung it on her back, and sent word back via a small cousin to her mother Hilaria that she was going with us. Dressed in ragged Tojolabal clothing, she was an angel in disguise. We could not have done it without her. As it was, the six and seven-year-olds cried most of the way on the trail. I could tell their little feet ached under the load of babies on their backs. Mid-way on that fifteen mile hike to Las Margaritas, Christina and I left the rest and later sent a truck back to bring them in. That night in our house that had felt too small for two people, we slept twenty-three people!

Although the timeline is unclear, it appears that by midweek, Julia, along with Antonio, Pancho, Ricardo, Enrique and some of the women, all returned to Jotana. With this little group was the government school inspector who had three official government documents affirming religious liberty for all Mexican citizens.

The night of our arrival, the school inspector called a town meeting. He did a magnificent job for us, and we marveled at his ability to keep order. However, at the door, as we were prepared to leave, the fury of hell broke loose and had it not been for the inspector; our men would have been killed. We knew to stay on was certain death. So on April 18, one month to the day of our men being beaten, we made our second exodus. The inspector accompanied us with a drawn pistol. It was a terrifically hot day, and we straggled into Las Margaritas heartsore and stunned.

After that incident, Julia appealed to the governor of the state who sent in soldiers to keep order. Red Brown of MAF, along with Bob Goerz from SIL, installed a two-way radio in Julia's house in Las Margaritas. "This," said Julia, "now allows me direct communication with those who can help."

The past week has been a full one. After the governor sent in soldiers, we received fresh news that helped us. However, it will still take time before our folks can go back to their homes. In the meantime, life here in Las Margaritas is far from dull. We have a fluctuating crowd, but always a crowd. Besides the people, we have four oxen, two horses, four pigs, a dog, a cat and some chickens. And we have not yet run out of floor space for any of the relatives who come to visit.

We cannot live without prayer. It must be our very life these days. It takes courage to go on. Legal battles are frustrating and wearying. However, Peggy and I feel that for the sake of Christ among the Tojolabals, we must see this through. So, our general prayer needs are for patience, good humor under crowded conditions, wisdom in decisions that must constantly be made, and refusal to be taken up with pesky prodding.

Looking up, *Julia*

Two months later, Julia wrote from Jotana saying that Pancho, Enrique, Victor and Antonio and their families could legally return to Jotana, but since their lives were still in danger, they were moving to the village of Chanchamajan.

I'll Just Say Hello.

Not only did Julia write engaging and humorous letters to her prayer and supporting partners, so too, did her co-worker, Peggy (Margaret) Wendell. On June 16, she began her letter as follows:

June 16, 1958

Every time I begin a form letter, I sit here trying to think of a new and scintillating salutation. All the standard forms, like Greetings! and Dear

Friends, somehow don't sound like me. Perhaps I should announce a contest for you all to enter your suggestions with the prize being a trip to Jotana during the next big fiesta. (I can assure you, you'd find excitement!) Well, I can't think of anything new and scintillating, so I'll go back to the familiar, Hello!

After her familiar greeting, Peggy said that, even though they were still living in Las Margaritas, they had learned that life in Jotana was a great deal calmer than it was two months before in April.

The crowd has thinned out. We're now down to six Tojolabals. This doesn't mean the believers have been allowed to go back to the village. However, they are finding new places to live. No, there have been no "Come-on-back-kids-we-were-only-fooling" offers made by the ringleaders of the persecution.

But we have an almighty God. In the midst of this persecution has come a tremendous blessing. His name is Pancho, and he appears to be God's gift to Julia and the translation program. He seems to have just the right knack of getting the Word of God into good idiomatic Tojolabal. If he were in the village, he would be spending his days working in his corn fields and too tired at night for headwork. But now he's here in Las Margaritas working on translation.

What's more, he loves God's Word and can hardly wait to discover new truths.

Although Peggy extolled Poncho's great ability as a co-Bible translator, she failed to mention his extraordinary journey into faith. In Julia's August letter to "Aaron and Hur," she corrected this omission with the following abridgment of Poncho's spiritual journey.

While being born into a calm well-ordered Tojolabal family, Pancho, the second son of Mateo and Maria's ten children, was never ordinary. From the beginning, Mateo and Maria realized they had a problem son on their hands. Pancho had a violent temper and a vile tongue. Without provocation, he would jump into the middle of a cooking fire, or break his father's machete, or smash whatever household goods were at hand. When he went fishing and the fish didn't bite, he would vehemently curse every Saint he could think of. He once broke off a finger of a family Saint and threw it into the fire. When no curse fell, and he was never ill, he felt freer than ever to go on his mad, willful way.

During his adolescence, his passions were unbridled. He had two jail terms for robbery. His parents insisted he bring the young girl he had shamed into the family, but that did not stop her pain of a grossly unfaithful husband. And then something happened. As quietly as a tuft carried by a gentle breeze, word got around that there was a religion that could make bad people good. Years before Poncho's Aunt Delfina had talked about this as she helped in the fields. But that phrase, "*a religion that made bad people good*" stuck in Poncho's mind. Then when the Christians began to talk about leaving Jotana, Pancho was suddenly jolted into realizing this would be his only chance. He had to ask the Christians how this could happen. If he didn't, he knew he could never be good.

More than anything, Pancho, wanted to be good, but didn't know how. When his mother learned of his desire, she was so delighted that the Lord might change him, she clasped her hands to think this wicked son of hers might be good. What followed was a chaotic sequence of temptations as one tumbled upon another. We prayed, we talked, always pointing him time after time to Jesus Christ the only one who could release him from the temptations of his past life.

Then several weeks after Pancho said he wanted the God who could make him good, a release came to his spirit. It is not necessary to go into the details of the enemy's fierce temptations. It's enough to say our Lord Jesus triumphed over all the forces of the enemy. Now day after day as Pancho and I sit at the translation table, I marvel as he takes the thoughts of God and recasts them into just the right kind of Tojolabal speech patterns. Clearly, Pancho has a gift with words. I now understand some of the answers as to the why of those fierce spiritual battles. Satan would love to have him, thus delaying and perhaps denying the message [of life] to Poncho's people. "But I have prayed for you." *That's* the difference. Does this strike a responsive chord?

Yours, by bonds of love, *Julia*

When he began his novel, *Dr. Zhivago*, for which he won the 1958 Nobel Prize for literature, Boris Pasternak said he wanted to write something that was "deep and true." All of her adult life, Julia's desire was to be a writer and she would eventually take time to hone her talent by taking a creative writing course. In the meantime, her burden was to give the Tojolabals a written word that was deep and true and beautiful, to give them *the* Book that could effect spiritual change and communicate God's offer of eternal life.

In October 1958, Julia wrote to tell her prayer partners that she was about to embark on a new adventure of faith. For about two years she had heard rumors of a group of Tojolabals living on the edge of the tribal area that "wanted to believe."[12] At first Julia was unsure if this were true, but when the group sent word that they wanted fifty hymnbooks and were preparing to build an airstrip, Julia "sat up." In her October letter she wrote:

---

[12] In the early fifties, the Mexican government opened up land in a national tropical forest for colonization. Many of the Tojolabals migrated from the Comitan-Jotana-Margaritas area to establish villages and begin a new life in this area.

This telling needs a defter pen, for God is apparently at work. "The wind bloweth where it listeth" and we are hearing the sound thereof and cannot yet "tell from whence it cometh and whither it goeth." Could this be the beginning of the answer to our prayers for a new day for the Tojolabals? If it is, we never thought it would begin in the dense jungle where malaria takes its toll. However, when our rigid attempts to impede the free and flexible flow of God's Spirit, we are left to own devices. What appears to be arbitrariness or even capriciousness in the operation of the Spirit is neither. This will be plain to us one day.

What was beyond Julia's expectation was that many Tojolabals in this region had come to faith through the witness of their near neighbors, the Tzeltals. And much like the Apostle Paul in Acts, Julia sought to offer her encouragement to the fledgling group by a personal visit. Like the Apostle Paul, Julia took along her Barnabas, only his name was Pancho. However, unlike the original Barnabas, Pancho took his whole family with him. A fellow SIL colleague, Viola Warkentin, also joined the company. Viola wrote that Julia "is an old hand at pioneering, and we are anticipating a grand time."

Before they made the trip to the lowland Tojolabal area, the little group traveled four days on horseback to set up a staging area in the Tzeltal village of Corralito. As noted previously, this was the village where the SIL translator and nurse team of Mariana Slocum and Florence Gerdel had established a thriving ministry.

Written from Corralitio

Late December 1958
Dear Aaron and Hur,

About 4 p.m. things are buzzing at our house in Corralito. Several of the clinic workers [that Florence has trained] came for writing lessons and others for arithmetic. One enterprising young man comes for Spanish and typing lessons.

On the morning of December 4, Pancho and five Tzeltal brethren set out for Tojolabal country. Before the day ended, Pancho was keenly aware his Tzeltal companions were equipped differently than was he. The Tzeltals are mountain people. Thus growing up on the perpendicular produces a larger heart, lungs and stronger leg muscles. The Tzeltal is a born mountain goat. The Tojolabal, on the other hand, is a born cowboy perfectly adapted for life on the flat dry high plains of his tribal area. When it comes time to sleep, a Tojolabal from the Jotana area looks for some kind of shelter. Not so a Tzeltal. He simply throws himself for rest on mother earth, be it wet or dry. Thus, a trip that ordinarily takes a Tzeltal two days, took this company six. But no one complained. They even carried Poncho's pack to help him along.

Time permitted Pancho to visit only five villages, most of whom were ready to believe. We know of eleven villages that are eagerly waiting to hear the Good News in their own tongue. In the village of Esperanza, a widow publicly threw her idol in the mud. This was a solemn and courageous act. In Rancho Alegre, a drunken religious fiesta was stopped, and people listened far into the night to how they could have a new life free from the burden of idolatry. In one village, a murderer begged for more teaching, and a shaman sat in rapt attention all day drinking in the Words of Life. Today at Santa María, all the men are gathered to measure an airstrip so that our cargo can go with them. We believe this promises to be the beginning of groups of families moving toward God. And this is the Spirit's method among people who are group minded. All of a sudden, I feel like Chicken Little, who thought the sky was falling on its tail. New believers must have God's Word and new hymn books and new primers and new tracts and new everything. We are working as much as possible. The Revised Gospel of Mark goes to the printer in January.

This Tzeltal interlude here in Corralito has been delightful. I saw their Christmas pageant for the first time. The whole story was portrayed by a cast of forty Tzeltals, all of whom were chosen by the church elders based on good conduct and clean living. One old wise man is a fine-looking ex-witchdoctor. As he presented his gift to the Christ child, I felt I was the happiest person in the world. It is people like *him* that we have presented to *Him*. They are our gold, frankincense and myrrh.

Joyfully yours, *Julia*

7

Jungle Living, 1959 – 60

The overriding story of 1959 centered on a fiery young
lawyer named Fidel Castro. On January 8, with
automobile horns honking, bells ringing and jubilant
crowds shouting, he, with his bearded revolutionary army
astride tanks and motor vehicles, entered Havana, Cuba to
begin a Marxist dictatorship.

On a lesser note to the public eye, but great in Kingdom
value, was the response by eager young people to be part of
world mission. In 1959, Wycliffe's membership went over
one thousand and the first second-generation member
joined the ranks as a Bible translator. That same year Julia,
now in her fortieth year, was once again pioneering. From
the tropical village of Santa María, Julia waited until June to
describe her new home and the lay of the land.

At Home in Santa María

> **Early June 1959**
>
> Dear Aaron and Hur,
>
> Our house is made with slender upright poles
> tied together with jungle vines. A tall palm-

thatch roof, an earth floor, furniture of poles and hand-hewn mahogany plank, a dash of gray plastic, a leisurely hammock on the porch—this is home in Santa María.

A month ago, after a reconnaissance by SIL colleague, Searle Hoogshagen, and MAF pilot, Floyd Bishop, Frances and I were landed at Rancho Chaparral where ten men, Tojolabals and Tzeltals, awaited our arrival. They, with our things on their backs, and we, accompanied by fellow SIL colleague, Hank Hershberger, set out for the village of Santa Maria. Four hours later we arrived at a fair size river which the Indians of the area had bridged by felling a tree and tying hand railings on the sides. After a good dip in the river, we began the steep climb up a more than a thousand-foot cliff. At times, we had to hoist ourselves by grabbing hold of small trees and vines by the trail side. That night two hot and exhausted missionary translators were glad to climb into our jungle hammocks. However, while we were indeed tired, the heat and jungle night noises made our sleep fitful.

For some years, the Tzeltals have been gossiping the good news of Jesus Christ to their near Tojolabal neighbors. Faithfully, steadily they prepared the ground until on Pancho's December 1958 trip, a small harvest awaited him. Then Pancho, at the urgent invitation of his

Tzeltal brethren, moved here in mid-March. The result is a Tzeltal-Tojolabal chapel with God's Word going forth in two languages. We are here to continue translation of Tojolabal scriptures, to carry on a simple medical ministry, to teach reading to the new brethren and to be of help in any way possible. Incidentally, Frances delivered a Tojolabal baby the first week and a Tzeltal baby on the second. No partiality there!

Just as hundreds of cross-cultural missionaries learned before her, including the Apostle Paul, Julia knew she was entering contested territory. She wrote:

We are in the stronghold of an enemy whose hold on men's souls is tenacious. After Pancho returned from his trip with the encouraging news that many people were eager to accept the Good News of the Gospel, we hoped and prayed that whole villages would turn to God. But what we have seen is an enemy who has snatched away some who at first eagerly received the Word. Alas, these have become its worst enemies. Others are indifferent. However, we happily report six new families who are attending the chapel services. Many of these have had a personal encounter with God.

Spiritual Battle in the Heavenlies

Julia ended her long letter with a nod to Paul's reminder in Ephesians 6:10ff that no matter how zealous she and

Frances were to be faithful witnesses for the Gospel, they needed outside help.

> We know we are fighting against the strategies of forces and authorities of the unseen world. And we believe such warfare is won by numbers of human spirits, placed side by side with the Holy Spirit, for victory over the enemy of the souls of men. The spiritual force is the prayer of many. Our Lord differentiated the strength of demons. Thus, some strongholds of Satan require more spiritual force to overthrow than others. Even Moses had to have human help to prevail. The Gospel worker on the foreign field must, likewise, have other spirits to aid him or her in the battle in the heavenlies. Explain it if you wish. It is a fact, and it works! I quote from Isobel Kuhn in *Nests Above The Abyss:* "What your part is entirely a matter between you and God."
>
>   Yours, here for Jesus' sake, *Julia*

At the bottom of her June letter was a P.S. paragraph written by Frances Jackson, who wrote the following to her praying partners:

> Because Julia has said the right things in the right way, I am sharing her letter with you. Lest you are wondering, "Aaron and Hur" refer to those friends of Moses, who held up his hands as he prayed for the battle. Your task is similar to that of those men of old. These last six weeks have

been exciting ones, and we are thankful for the way the Lord has provided abundantly for this new venture.

One of the adventures Frances referred to was getting used to the new experience of jungle living and the plethora of "creepy-crawlies."

Annoyances

Late July 1959
Dear Aaron and Hur,

Jungle living has been a new experience for us. At first, we doubted we'd live to tell the story. There were ants, all kinds of them, and everywhere. An army of them moved us out of our beds one night. Then came the bees. They pestered us to death. Cockroaches were contaminating our food and dishes and greedily devouring our books and clothes. Rats, several dozens of them, ruled the place by night. Then rains of May brought mosquitoes, and the tiniest little fierce-biting flies. A flash flood inundated our dirt floor and turned it to mud. Mildew and rust set in. For a month, the heat was so oppressive that without a refrigerator, I felt life was not worth living. Pigs piled up on the porch to sleep and shook the house when they scratched their backs. Physical battles were so pressing that the battles of the spirit seemed secondary.

However, gradually things began to look up.
MAF brought some good ant poison, and we
haven't had any since. We got our propane gas
tanks tightened, and the bees disappeared.
Government men came and sprayed our house
and thousands of cockroaches died. Good traps
and poison killed off most of the rats. Nets
protect us from mosquitoes and insect repellent
from flies. Time and sunshine dried up the floor;
rains have brought the temperature down. We
got a fence to keep the pigs out. Life is rosy.

Annoyances
Those little prickly things
That gather great momentum
And put big things on the fringe,
Deliver, Lord, from panic
Make the grotesque small.
And before I see the answer.
Let me thank thee for them All.

Yours, for Jesus' sake, *Julia*

Translation Workshops

In an earlier letter, Julia introduced her prayer partners to
the internal structure of the Mexico SIL branch. She gave
high praise to her SIL teammates who worked quietly
behind the scenes serving with efficiency and good will.
Julia was especially grateful to those working in the finance
office who kept the hundreds of financial accounts in
order. And after she had spent time working in the

publications department, she was impressed with the high-quality production of primers, dictionaries, gospels and other materials being readied for a variety of ethnic languages. Julia also lauded the then Mexico SIL director, Dr. Benjamin (Ben) Elson, and the member-staffed executive committee who shared the burden of directing the growing demands of the Mexico branch.

In 1960, one of the burdens uppermost in Ben Elson's mind was the quality and low production of New Testament translations. When Ben first became director, he wondered why many of the members were failing to get their work accomplished. At one point, he even considered putting such people on discipline. But Ben began to understand that, rather than discipline, they needed practical help. As he explained:

> I began to reflect on how frustrated I had been
> during the time I was translating. The reason was
> I didn't have anyone with whom to talk over my
> translation problems. I realized all our workers
> needed help. They needed it in translation,
> literacy, and linguistics, and as director it was my
> duty to do something about it.[13]

Ben Elson's solution was to appoint John Beekman as the Branch's official Translation Consultant.[14] John had

---

[13] Hugh Steven. *The John Beekman Story, The Man With The Noisy Heart* (Chicago: Moody Press, 1979) pp. 78-79.

[14] Impressed with John's accomplishment in developing innovative Bible translation principles and inspiring and helping other translators

pioneered and helped several of his colleagues understand the concept of "meaningful" or idiomatic translation. Often, the translations being produced were word for word or adhered too closely to the linguistic structure of the original text, even though the result did not conform to the natural way in which people spoke their language. To avoid a wooden or stilted translation, John Beekman stressed that the resulting work should read like a great piece of literature in the target language. And to accomplish this, a translator needed to master both the culture and language of the ethnic group and absorb their unique characteristics. The goal is to capture the spirit and meaning of the text and translate it into the idiomatic speech patterns natural to the target language community.

By 1961 a new translation center in Ixmiquilpan in central Mexico was fully operational. Here a translator, with his or her language helpers and co-translators, could receive concentrated help to find solutions to many of the complex technical translation problems. Over the years, this center and John Beckman's translation workshops were to have a profound and revolutionary effect on the quality and speed of Bible translation, not only for the Mexico branch but throughout the entire world of Wycliffe and beyond.

There were many translators who, after participating in a workshop, said things like: "I have learned more about translation principles and procedures here at this workshop

to continue a difficult task, the Wycliffe Board of Directors eventually appointed him to the newly created post of International Translator Coordinator.

in three months than I learned in the past ten years."[15] By the late fifties and early sixties, Julia was aware of the benefits of attending a translation workshop and in April 1960, she wrote:

> Dear Aaron and Hur,
>
> For the last few years, we have wanted to attend a translation workshop. But, if you recall, we've been so busy being persecuted that we just couldn't work it in between blows. Then a year ago we moved to our new jungle home. So this is the first year that we could attend. Colleagues who have attended these translation conferences and workshops tell us how very helpful they are. One thing of which I am certain is that they succeeded in letting me know that one doesn't know as much as one thinks one knows. And knowing that you don't know as much as you think you know is a tremendous stride forward in the translation process. I am sure I'll learn how to recognize problems, but we shall work on solutions as well. All to the glorious end goal of giving the ethnic people of Mexico the Word of God that really speaks their language.

After spending two "profitable" months at the

---

[15] For examples of the kinds of problems a Bible translator must solve, see Appendix A.

translation conference in Mitla,[16] Julia and her company of Tojolabal language helpers took a side trip to the coastal city of Salina Cruz on the gulf of Tehuantepec. For Pancho, his wife Cayetana and the others, it was a never-to-be-forgotten experience.

Late June 1960
Dear Aaron and Hur,

Nothing in their wildest imaginations prepared the little company of Tojolabals for seeing this vast body of restless water for the first time. Huge crabs sunned themselves on the boulders that reinforced the pier. Large fish flung themselves in happy abandonment out of the water. Small fishing vessels were offloading baskets of iced shrimp. Mexico's Miguel Aleman was in dock. Then, to end a most perfect day, the group had a ride on the merry-go-round. That they were the only adults gliding around on their trusty steeds seemed not to embarrass them in the least. We returned to the town of Juchitán weary but contented.

After the group parted company (the Tojolabals to Comitán), Julia returned to Santa María. In a letter written in late June, Julia said she returned with a renewed alertness of needing to depend on the Holy Spirit for any forward

---

[16] The SIL center in the town of Mitla, Oaxaca was an alternative workshop site just prior to the Ixmiquilpan center's opening in 1961.

movement among the Tojolabals. What troubled Julia was living in close proximity to the Tzeltals, who had a hunger for God, while the Tojolabals were mostly apathetic about the gospel.

Dear Aaron and Hur,

Santa María is right on the border of Tzeltal and Tojolabal country. We are assigned to the latter, but find ourselves being assimilated by the former. We desperately desire to move further "inland" among the Tojolabals but before this can happen, they must invite us. In the meantime, medicine and scarcity of corn have brought numbers from other Tojolabal villages to Santa Maria. Pancho and Ramon continue to be a faithful witness. The Word of God is being preached as Tojolabal records are being played in a number of villages. Yet the Tojolabals are not moving toward God.

I ask myself, are we failing to find that special redemptive key that will meet their particular spiritual need? When Pancho and Ramon present the gospel, they listen with apparent interest but go away, one after another, seemingly unmoved by the truths that are our very breath and life. It is deadening apathy. The contrast is even more glaring alongside the Tzeltals who have moved by the thousands to the love of God. This has caused much soul-searching on our part.

I don't share this for sympathy, but for prayer. Psalm 74 and others like it are meat and drink for us these days. After a list of discoursing events, the Psalmist cries, "Why dost thou hold back thy hand, why dost thou keep thy right hand in thy bosom?" Then, in glad reflection, "Yet God, my King, is from old, working salvation in the midst of the earth." These ancient words give us courage to keep on keeping on.

One area of encouragement is the two reading classes for the teenagers. They are the eager-beaver kind that usually pop-up before class time. They gobble up every lesson, which keeps Frances, their teacher, out of breath trying to revise a second primer for them. One of the differences between working in Comitán and here in the jungle of Santa María is that we go to bed every night at 7:30. Nocturnal mosquitoes are crazy for white meat. And getting under our mosquito nets is the only safe place to be. It's interesting how much work one can do under a net!

In His glad service, *Julia*

A young girl in a typical Tojolabal blouse, circa 1944.

Julia shows a picture book to a young Tojolabal boy, who is babysitting his younger sister, circa 1944.

Julia and short term co-worker Celia Douglas, circa 1944.

*A Tojolabal woman carrying a clay water jug,
circa 1944.*

A Tojolabal boy twisting fiber of the maguey (or century) plant to make string or a strong thread, circa 1944.

Co-worker Frances Jackson conducts an early Tojolabal children's literacy class, circa 1950.

Julia and Tojolabal language helper Enrique make use of the reel to reel tape recorder for language learning. This was high technology in the early 1950s.

A Tojolabal oxcart, circa 1944.

A young Tojolabal man relaxes with his guitar, circa. 1951.

A young Tojolabal woman, circa 1950.

*A Tojolabal man drying fibers of the maguey plant, circa 1950.
The fibers may be used to make rope, matting and coarse cloth.*

The maguey plant also makes
an excellent clothesline,
circa 1944.

Co-worker Peggy Wendell draws
water from Julia's backyard well,
circa 1951.

A maguey field in San Andres, circa 1957. In addition
to fiber for rope and matting, the plant produces
"honey water."

Pedro Hernández Jiménez, here wearing a Tojolobal fiesta shirt, is part of a dedicated team of educated young men currently working on the revision of the Tojolobal New Testament.

8

Living on Borrowed Time, 1961 – 64

Wherever Julia lived, Jotana, Comitán, Las Margaritas, and Santa María, each had come to represent different and often conflicting values; each had their own unique utility. Comitán was a place to rest and regroup. Las Margaritas was a city of refuge. Jotana was a place of both challenge and hostility. Since there was ongoing persecution directed against the evangelical Christians, Julia found the continual unrest counterproductive to her goal of translating the Tojolabal New Testament. After living in Santa Maria for almost four years, 1959-1962, Julia had this to say in her October 1962 letter:

Written From Jungle Camp

Dear Aaron and Hur,

I have just finished a stint of being the caretaker (in the off season) of Jungle Camp. There are several angles from which I could approach this subject, but to make me sound a little famous: I am the first maiden lady, or any kind of lady, they've ever left in charge. History might prove me to be the last. To make a comparison, suppose you'd go away from July to October and leave your farm in complete charge of a woman scarcely able to tell a cow from a horse.

I got into this predicament because I was here on the spot. This is how it happened. In March, I got the bright idea that moving to Jungle Camp would solve some of my problems, one of which was not having enough concentrated time to work on translation while living in Santa María. I was able to convince our director, a man of unusual discernment, and he gave me the go-ahead. Thus, on March 8 of this year, several planeloads of us and our stuff flew the fifteen minutes over three mountain ranges to Jungle Camp.

Little did we know that shortly after our arrival an assortment of twenty Tojolabals would join us. A few weeks after their arrival, the group expanded with the birth of three new babies. Each family has their own mud hut. I share a small hut with Angela, a wonderful Tojolabal widow. She is a delight to have around, partly because it helps tremendously to have Tojolabal phonemes floating around day and night. Now, she and I are working on 1 Corinthians.

I hope you're praying about translation, not just this Tojolabal one, but this sort of thing is going on all over the world. I've got a sneaking feeling this worldwide Bible translation movement is terrifically significant. Someday, we might discover it's more so than rockets and spacemen and sputniks. And it's really exciting to be a part of it.

Yours, at His orders, *Julia*

P.S To complete the domestic scene, we have two cats and several toads. At night the latter come uninvited to feast on the smaller wild life flying around our Coleman lantern.

It's unclear if it was by design or because not all of Julia's letters have been preserved, but there is a three-month blank between October 1962 and February 1963 and then not another word until January 12, 1964. And then, to the surprise of Julia's partners, the January 12 letter, written by an unnamed amanuensis, was calling Julia's friends and partners to a special session of prayer on her behalf.

She Needs Much Prayer

January 12, 1964
Dear Aaron and Hur,

This letter is being written by a friend of Julia Supple's. For several weeks, she has been too ill to write and has asked me to inform you. At the end of September, Julia left Mexico to begin a short furlough to visit her mother and friends in California, Oregon and Arizona. After which she had planned to return to Mexico in February in time to attend a translation workshop in Ixmiquilpan. She had experienced good progress in getting the Tojolabal New Testament completed in a first draft.

Her mother had purchased a car for her [her first], and Julia began her furlough learning how to drive. She then went on an extended speaking trip with her mother from Oxnard, California to Salinas, California, Portland, Central Point, Oregon and Cave Junction. While she was in Portland, she had much pain and discomfort and thought she had picked up a stomach-flu bug. When the pain continued, and after consultation with a doctor, she felt it necessary to have a complete checkup. She then drove herself to the Loma Linda hospital in California.

She arrived at Loma Linda on December 21 but was unable to get an appointment until January 7. Rather than stay alone in a hotel during the holidays, she drove to Phoenix, Arizona. Julia returned to Loma Linda on the 27th and after a series of tests, she underwent serious major surgery on January 10 to remove two large tumors, one of which was malignant. Julia has a positive attitude, and she also has a good appetite. However, when she came out of the operating room, her doctor said, "She needs much prayer."

For Julia Supple

P.S. The Mexico office informs us that Julia was released from the hospital on January 21. She is making good progress but stands in need of continued prayer.

The mystery of who wrote the January 12 letter was finally revealed in Julia's upbeat February 23, 1964 letter in which she wrote:

Dear Aaron and Hur,

Some of you were confused about who wrote the January 12th letter. The body of the letter was written by my good friend Edith Dunnam. The letter was printed and mailed from our Mexico City offices. The P.S. was added by persons unknown.

Of all the gifts of His love during the pre-and post-surgery days, perhaps Edith and Lois Hall were the dearest. Edith has opened her heart and home to me. It is here I am finding new strength and the sheer joy of living again. I soak up the warm Arizona sun on her back patio. Lois Hall is a perfect nurse and has watched over me with TLC. Lois usually teaches school in Salinas, California but is presently on a leave of absence.

This entire experience was unplanned by any of us but perfectly planned by Him. This has all been a new experience. I've been a healthy specimen all my adult life. But now I know a little bit about life on the horizontal, and I trust it will make me a more understanding and tender person. I now appreciate more fully what the Presbyterians call the Common Grace—grace given by God and shared commonly by humanity. I would include all the fine doctors and nurses who ease our pains so unselfishly and give themselves to make us more comfortable.

For a woman with a capacity for the fullness of living, Julia's post-operative schedule included twice weekly swimming and daily walks of several blocks. From her letters, her partners knew her as a woman with a persistent hope and confidence in her Lord to work out His will in her life and ministry. And although she was positive and optimistic and had "heart ease" about her eventual recovery, she acknowledged she was living on borrowed time. In her uncharacteristically long February 23 letter, she wrote:

Volumes of prayer ascended for me when I needed it most. Without doubt, this is one reason why I've made such a quick comeback. We all know this disease is tricky. So there is still room for much prayer for me, and I am asking you to continue steadfast, not doubting. Even though I have to face the decision of further treatments, which are known to harm the body, by His grace, I have heart ease about the whole matter. As I was praying and contemplating this, a lovely verse came by mail. It's by Alice Hanche Mortenson, and the words ministered to my heart and gave me perfect rest in leaving the future in God's hands alone.

> I Live On Borrowed Time
> I have been healed, not instantly,
> But through a surgeon's skill;
> God often uses human hands to
> Carry out His will.
> So I thank Him more, not less,
> For every trying hour
> That made me draw unceasingly
> On His unfailing power.
> I thank Him, yes, for nights of pain
> When heaven seemed to bend
> Above my bed with songs of praise
> And God Himself would send
> Such sweet assurance to my soul.
> Such evidence of care,
> That, though I could not see his face,
> I knew that He was there.
> So I rise again to serve
> And I live on "borrowed time."
> I pray that I shall not forget
> My days are His, not mine.

Although Julia was keenly aware of her mortality, she was determined to live an intentional life of spiritual and intellectual discovery. She refused to allow the amorphous specter of death to determine how she would continue to live out her life and ministry. The last paragraph of her letter is a clear indication of this resolve.

> I've just read the delightful little book *Your God is Too Small* by J.B. Phillips. He is discussing the kind of people who think God is a disappointment and says, "To recall God's unfaithfulness appears to give them the same ghoulish pleasure that others find in recounting the grisly details of their operations." I smiled at that and determined this letter would be it— we're going to leave the grisly details behind and press on to the high calling of God in Christ Jesus!
>
> Joyfully His, body, soul and spirit, *Julia*

One of Julia's trademark dictums was: "My work among the Tojolabals is so utterly absorbing; I wouldn't change places with anyone." However, in her April 1964 letter, written from Phoenix; she allowed that her sanguine view of her ministry predated her ownership of a 1958 Rambler she named "Effie."

> Dear Aaron and Hur,
>
> You all know for years I've been totally absorbed with my work among the Tojolabal people, and that continues to be true. But just in case you think I'm too disgustingly well adjusted, I hasten to assure you that certain situations in life bother me. For instance, like buying a utility trailer. Was

it not for some sound advice from various male acquaintances, I might well have ended up in disaster somewhere down the road about 150 miles from the nearest service station. I'd be the last one to know that trailers need to be balanced or that gas refrigerators are transported upright, not lying down. In fact, on several occasions, the men of my life have kept me from complete shambles.

Julia's April letter was to inform her prayer partners that she, along with her friend Lois Hall and her newly acquired car and utility trailer, were to depart for Mexico by mid-May. But in-mid July her partners received another letter, written not from Mexico, but still from Phoenix, Arizona.

Mid-July 1964
Dear Aaron and Hur,

I've told you how concerned I've been about having to drive through Mexico City's mad traffic without a complete nervous collapse, to say nothing of being totally splattered all over the area. Well, it has turned out that I was worrying too soon. We have been delayed, and the little rambler has played a major role in that delay.

At the risk of boring you, let me recount some of the highlights missionaries call "furlough." I've always felt every middle-aged woman should do something to spice up one's life. So the

Rambler was my outlet. The car was a gift from my mother, and since I had never driven a car before, I took driving lessons to the tune of eight dollars an hour. When the time grew near to take my driver's test to get my driver's license, I faced a high psychological hurdle. Finally, in desperation, my non-religious teacher reminded me I was, after all, a missionary and missionaries are supposed to have faith, and he supposed that faith should operate for such a mundane thing as being able to pass a driver's test. Well, I got mad (at myself, of course) and passed it.

Rethinking My Life

Included in my furlough plans was the idea of taking some writing courses. But my study plans were unexpectedly interrupted by a surgery that you already know about. As a consequence of cancer, I re-thought my life in terms of getting my job done as soon as possible. When I was in the hospital, I decided to expedite the translation of the Tojolabal New Testament by moving from an extreme pioneer situation of jungle life into the more agreeable climate and semi-civilization of the little village of Las Margaritas. When I wrote Pancho of my plans, he wrote back some time later and said, "I've found you a lovely house, it has a floor and running water."

In the meantime, all wasn't well with "Effie." Julia

reported that her neighborhood mechanic gloomily predicted her Rambler was in need of serious repairs.

When I heard this, I trustingly committed the car to a garage that advertised on Christian radio as having mechanics that were Christians. However, I was shocked when they told me I needed to have a rebuilt engine to the tune of three hundred dollars. Since I was without experience in such matters, I told them to go ahead.

Later when the repairs were completed, Julia, as naive as she was about the nature of cars, understood enough to know that something was still wrong with the car when she saw black smoke belching from the exhaust. When Julia returned to the garage to complain, it happened to be on the morning when the garage business was going into receivership, and nobody would take responsibility for her repairs.

At the bottom of her long letter, Julia included a cartoon of a grease-stained mechanic leaning over the engine of a car saying to the lady customer, "If this were a horse, I'd advise you to shoot it." And that's just about what Julia decided to do.

The ups and downs and ins and outs of the days that followed are not necessary to retell but when I saw this cartoon, I had to laugh since it graphically expressed my sentiments. I have several escape mechanisms to use for coping with frustration. My most used is sleep. But this deal has been so long and drawn out that I would have had to develop sleeping sickness. So it wasn't hard to leave this whole mess in Edith Dunnam's unfailing hands, and I went to California.

Actually, it wasn't to escape that Julia and her friend Lois Hall went to California. Lois needed a teaching position for fall and she wanted to explore various teaching options.

Lois had planned to be with me in Mexico for the summer before going back to teaching school in the fall. But with the Rambler complications, I began to feel it was Balaam's ass and surely the Angel of the Lord was in the way hindering us. There was sweet evidence of the Lord's blessing during our seventeen-day trip. We began in San Diego and went all the way to San Francisco interviewing educators. We had a very good trip.

But, oh, the grim reality on our return to Phoenix, there sat the Rambler, big as life. Everything the mechanics did to the car only worsened the condition. Someone wisely advised, "Sell the critter before you spend more money on it." I reluctantly agreed since it would be folly to start out on the long road to Mexico in such a poor vehicle pulling a luggage trailer. So now "Effie" has a for-sale sign on it.

Asking Ultimate Questions

One of the ultimate questions any thoughtful and reflective Christian can ask is how to discover the fingerprints of God in the fog and fragmentation of one's life experience. Then there's the question posed by Elizabeth Vining, author of *Windows for the Crown Prince*, to consider. *"In living our lives, how much of the pivotal decisions that come into our lives shall we leave in God's hands?"* After Julia had come to terms with what, for her, was the loss of a sizable amount of money, she wrote a remarkable answer to the two above questions.

> I hope you are still with me, if you are not, take a deep breath and hear me through. When I saw the For Sale on the Rambler, my first reaction was, so what? Now is the time to practice what I preach that THINGS aren't important anyway so why not push them all over a cliff and get on my way back to Mexico! A good night's sleep calmed me down somewhat and some heart-searching and prayer alone and corporately began to make things look like this.
>
> 1. The Rambler had been a gift from Him. It was, furthermore, an Ephesians 3:20 kind of gift, since I hadn't ever thought of owning a car.
>
> a. Mother and I had a grand trip to Oregon. Thank you, Lord.
>
> b. It was a boost to a middle-age morale. Thank you, Lord.

c. There was fun in every mile. Thank you, Lord.

d. I had supposed this car had been given to help expedite the translation of the New Testament. We shall have to transport our translation helper and his family thousands of miles in the next few years. Thank you, Lord, for having something better in mind for us.

e. The Lord giveth and the Lord taketh away. Blessed be the name of the Lord.

2. I must utterly ignore second causes. In the final analysis, I must deal with God alone. This takes care of bitterness and frustration and saves doctor bills on migraine headaches, tense neck muscles and colitis.

Furthermore, to harrow my soul over the $300.00 "down the drain" is not the will of God. My failure of good judgment is confessed to the Father, and He has forgiven. It is no effort for Him, if He pleases, to supply me with a new car or if not, His withholding will bring a happier solution. There is an eternal truth involved here. He means only the best for His children.

Never Think God's Delays Are God's Denials.

3. I must not "dump" the trailer and its contents because they, too, were gifts from God. Therefore, I conclude that He has some solution in store for me in eventually transporting them

to Mexico. They will, in the meantime, remain in Phoenix. *"Never think that God's delays are God's denials. Hold fast, hold out. Patience is genius. If there be no enemy, no fight, if no fight, no victory, if no victory, no crown"* (Savonarola).

4. There is no other way forward. I am repacking the essentials and plan to be on my way to Nogales and south by train. In view of the turn of events, it doesn't seem wise for Lois to go along.

Words can be so empty, but for the discerning I know there are some content in the recounting of these happenings. It is never pleasant to be pushed into "wit's" corner, but it is good for us. I have had to reevaluate and rethink several planks in the platform of my life philosophy. And I'm more convinced than ever *that we are in bondage to whatever we cannot part with. Only the eternal matters. The spiritual world is the real world. There is terrain there still to be discovered, peaks yet to be scaled, precious truth to be mined. Material things take their right place in life only as they have a proper relationship to the spiritual. To maintain this perspective, our Father many times must bring us to the place where we can pray the Prayer of Relinquishment.*

Yours, most sincerely in Christ, *Julia*

If it had happened a month or so later, Julia might (perhaps with some pride) have assumed it was her letter that God used to awaken friends to her need for transportation. But, in fact, it happened just two days after she had sent her lengthy letter to Mexico for printing and mailing.

Thus, in her mid-September 1964 letter, she wanted it to be absolutely clear that the promise of Isaiah 65:24[17] came true for her in ways that defied human reasoning. In that short one-page letter, she asked her praying friends and partners to rejoice with her for the unexpected gift of a new 1964 Chevrolet Station Wagon, ermine white with red interior. With tongue-in-cheek, she said she might have preferred a different interior, but not so the Tojolabals. "They like any color, just so it's red," she said.

Dear Aaron and Hur,

As an adult I've often wished to recapture that sparkling feeling of a child on Christmas morning. [A few days ago] this was one time I almost did. I have to say the gradual unfolding of our Lord's kind plan for me in these days has been a shining thing. His love has found surprising and ever widening expressions in the love shown through many new friends. This gift [of a new station wagon] was from them.

I still feel wide-eyed at their spiritual audacity of such generosity toward one they barely know. If

---

[17] "I will answer them before they even call to me. While they are still talking about their needs, I will go ahead and answer their prayers" (New Living Translation).

I could suddenly be transformed into Saint Theresa, it would help. But I'm uneasily awaiting the thud when they discover how very human I really am.

Julia continued in her letter to tell how she, with her eighty-year-old mother, took a small motor trip around Portland. She also informed her partners that her mother was planning to return to Mexico with her. To alleviate all fears that the trip must be too difficult for her mother, Julia informed her partners that at age sixteen her mother had moved to Oklahoma via covered wagon. Further, she let it be known her mother had lived in a house dug out of the earth with the roof just above the ground. And in case her friends were worried about unpleasant "critters" in Mexico, Julia added that her mother once found a rattlesnake in the coils of her bedsprings. "So," said Julia, "missionary life in Mexico will be mother's milk in comparison to her pioneer days." Julia then ended her letter with yet another insightful reflection on the journey of faith and life.

I think it is a mistake to think of God's intervention in terms of unusual events and dramatic happenings. These past weeks have held a number of these for me but most of my days are full of ordinary events, common experiences. Are we to believe God is not interested in these? I think not. So in the commonplace of this waiting interim, I purpose to practice the art of listening to the inner Voice with regard to small matters. And somehow, some way or other, God does put a shining wonder into the lives of those who have listening hearts. This must be His adult functional substitute for the starry-eyed childhood experience. "Look to Him and be radiant" are the ancient words of Psalm 34:5.

Yours, most sincerely in Christ, *Julia*

9

A Half Century Letter, 1919 – 1969

It's fair to say that from 1964 to 1969, the Western world was caught-up in the heady enthusiasm of revolutionary cultural and social changes. There was the Hippie Summer of Love in 1967. This was balanced by the most watched family film of all time, *The Sound of Music*.

After the 1967 explosion of the Six-Day War in the Middle East came the Vietnam Tet Offensive in 1968. However, there was also the winter Olympics that year when the world watched a graceful Peggy Fleming become a beloved figure skating champion. And then there was Neil Armstrong, that all-American man, who took a giant step for mankind and the world of science when he left his footprint on the moon.

What is curious about this moment in time is that while Julia was living an isolated life in an obscure village in Southern Mexico, she was aware of these cultural and social upheavals and called her partners to pray as Jeremiah (29:7) did "for the peace of the city." In an October 1968 letter to "Aaron and Hur," she wrote:

> While I spend most of my time working and struggling over the exegesis of some New Testament passage as I sit at a translation desk, I'm happy to be alive. But while I am enjoying the beauty of the warm rich colors of fall and the goodness and love of God, I am also aware I am a person in a world on the skids. I am asking God to make me effectually related to it. I worry about Hippies and Yuppies and the Democratic Convention and the Supreme Court, unconcerned Christians and race riots. But I also know these conditions are transitory and my worries about them must be, too. I look forward to the time when the Lord will bare his arm before the eyes of all nations.

What is also interesting about this letter is that Julia knew who she was and what her responsibility before God was to a group of preliterate people. At the same time, she knew the importance of living an examined life in relation to her calling and to her Lord and the larger world. Thus, on the occasion of her upcoming fiftieth birthday on February 14, 1969, she paused to give a retrospective view of her life, half of which she had lived cross-culturally.

Dear Aaron and Hur,

In Catherine Marshall's *Christy*, Aunt Polly is quoted as saying, "When my eighteenth you'un was birthed on my fiftieth nameday, just took a notion to drapp all such ou'tn my head. Birthdays are just a botheration."

Aunt Polly and I part ways here. My fiftieth nameday is coming up, and I actually feel quite exhilarated. Folks who've made it through a half century deserve a hearing! So I thought maybe I'd make this missive a patchwork of this and that, hoping to strike a few responsive chords about that thing we all have in common—living.

It is impossible to recognize all who've been responsible for building into our lives the philosophies we accumulate, or to enumerate the things that jell life-ideas for us. Contributing factors are too many and sometimes come so quickly that we scarcely know what has happened. But those wise men we currently call psychiatrists tell us much of what we are come from what our parents gave us.

What my father left me would be genetically given because I was only a babe when he died. He was a farm boy from Kansas. His stock was not too far back from County Cork, Ireland. My mother sprang from Kentucky mountain stock where family pride and dignity were often protected by long feuding. Almost to her death, my mother could hold the younger set of the family spellbound by relating the gory details of how Uncle Clem was riddled by bullets by his half brothers.

My great grandmother wore toe sacks[18] and smoked a corncob pipe. She liked to tell about the religious ecstasy they experienced in their little Christian church in the mountains. She said, "we were so happy in the Lord. We would dance all around the outside aisles, clapping and singing."

Long before my older sister Lela and I knew that Christ was our enabler, mother told us "that to want to attain, was to be able to attain." And she was continually telling us to never say "can't." When she died, my sister Lela said, "Julia, even though it was difficult for her to express love, we know we were loved." And we did. Through hard work and careful managing, Mother gave us a childhood of complete security. She beamed when we excelled; she sympathized when we failed. She was creative, had a flare for interior decorating, painted China and won seventy prizes for writing in contest entries. Our yard was always a riot of color with a corner for a few vegetables. On the perimeter of her list of God's common graces was the cacti family.

I probably inherited my love for new ex-periences from my mother. As a girl she moved in a wagon train from Illinois to the panhandle

---

[18] "Toe" or "tow" refers to the waste fibers of flax, jute or hemp. A tow sack (also called a gunny sack) is thus a coarse fibered bag or sack. A more general term is simply a burlap bag.

of Oklahoma. It never bothered her to break up housekeeping and move. She just held a rummage sale to pare down our possessions and off we went again. So the ambulation of the missionary life hasn't been the trauma to me as to others whose stock gathered about them antiques and old lace.

And now for more than half of these fifty years I've had a love affair going with the offspring of the ancient Maya. It probably started when I had a serious meeting with Jesus Christ and slowly began to comprehend His passion for the world. That happened in my early high school days. After which came Bible School, and five years work at Western Union. Then came the choice of a mission for me. Wycliffe Bible Translators was a good fit for me. The organization allowed elbow room for people like me who can't be smothered. The group isn't stuffy or pedantic. Neither does it turn out production-line people. Perhaps a weakness is that it is too patient with folks like me who have taken so long to produce a New Testament.

I would like to talk to you a bit about this, too. The beginning years among the Tojolabals were years of digging, almost bare-handed, into an unwritten language from reticent people. A tool had been placed in our hands, but at the time it was a blunt tool. Its name is linguistics. I was one of the generations which floundered around.[19] I finally translated but did not publish because my New Testament was too literal, too stilted and stiff. It did not communicate well to the reader.

Then slowly I and others began to realize that Bible translation is a science, as well as linguistics, and a very exciting one. It involves years of intimacy with people, absorbing their original thought patterns, their life philosophies. It has the heartbeat of involvement in the pathos and verve of another culture. A good translator must know how to remold the meaning of the original text into the folksiness and normal everyday speech patterns of the receptor language.

The translation should scintillate with idioms characteristic of each individual ethnic language, making it so much the reader's own that Jesus Christ can walk out of the pages right into the heart of the individual. The production of the final manuscript is not a sterile thing. It is the handiwork of sound scholarship coupled with fertile imagination and the involvement of a great number of supporting group team members and, of course, one's Aaron and Hur partners.

---

[19] See Chapter Seven on Translation Workshops and the breakthrough on new Bible translation methods.

> In 1969, barring unforeseen circumstances, we should see the Tojolabal New Testament finished for the second time (this time with the folksiness embedded in the text) and ready for printing. It then follows proofreading and the grind part of the process. And all the time, at my side are faithful Tojolabal brethren without whose help the translation would be a farce.

One of the involvements Julia failed to mention in her half-century retrospective was her growing fondness for Panchita and Delfina. During the early part of 1967, Julia spent six weeks at the Ixmiquilpan translation center. There, under the watchful eyes of expert consultants, Julia worked through some of the more difficult New Testament books. With her were Delfina, who, said Julia, was a "perfect translation helper." Delfina's seven-year-old daughter Panchita and Delfina's younger brother Manuel[20] were also there.

Part of Julia's story among the Tojolabals involves more than academic Bible translation. Her story is also about interweaving her life with the lives of the Tojolabal people. Two of these were, of course, Delfina and Panchita. After Julia's mother died in August 1967, Julia decided to remain in Santa Ana, California, then the location of the headquarters of Wycliffe Bible Translators. With Julia were Delfina and Panchita. It was Julia's plan to continue

---

[20] I regret not having the last names of these and other Tojolabals who were important co-translators of the Tojolabal New Testament.

working on translation while waiting to be enrolled for a second translation workshop in February 1968.

In one of her letters, Julia mentioned that while Panchita was age seven, she wore a size four clothing. Over the years Delfina and Panchita had become like family to Julia. In September, Julia wrote:

> Dear Aaron and Hur,
>
> Panchita begins first-grade tomorrow, and she is most excited. That excitement hit white heat when we bought her a pretty little lunch box with a thermos bottle. Today, she told a new friend, "I'm from Mexico. I'm a Mayan Indian!" Then she wanted to know what "you're a precious little girl" meant! English she has taken in her stride, and the teacher told us she is always the center of attention. However, to keep her in line, I've heard her being told by her mother more than once, "Now just be quiet, dear, because I'm not one bit impressed with your importance."

Then in her "Almost August 1968" letter, Julia filled in some of Delfina's and Panchita's story.

> Dear Aaron and Hur,
>
> What I want to talk about is Panchita. She matters a lot in our lives because she, being the daughter of our dear Delfina, belongs. At the beginning, Panchita was an unwanted child.

Delfina had been forced by her parents to marry her husband and when they separated eleven months later, she was pregnant. So little Panchita was born in Delfina's family home. Her first year was plagued by severe illness, and once in desperation, Delfina laid her aside to die. A few days later, Delfina, with a scrap of child in her arms, bereft of human consolation and crying until no tears were left, had that quiet revelation of Jesus Christ that she was indeed loved. And in response, as Mary of old, she broke her alabaster box, giving Him the very dearest of her love gifts, this tiny sickly babe. That was seven years ago. And almost effortlessly He brought our lives together so that she could be an instrument to make the Tojolabal New Testament just what it should be for her people.

During the time Julia lived in Santa Ana, California, she occasionally took speaking engagements in local-area churches. Part of Julia's program was to have Delfina give her testimony, of how she had come to faith in Jesus Christ. And often Panchita was introduced as well. On one of these engagements at a church in Anaheim, Panchita's life took a dramatic turn.

Dear Aaron and Hur,

It was there we met Joan and Dick Shimeall and their three children. The last mad day of packing for us to return to Mexico, the Shimealls offered to take her into their family and send her to school.

For Panchita to remain in the U.S. would, in Julia's words, be Delfina's decision and would require cutting through thick bundles of red tape. What followed were months of hard thinking, soul-searching and diplomatic negotiations that involved the American Embassy in Mexico City and the legal authorities in Panchita's hometown of Las Margaritas and Comitán. After Julia's promise to stand by Delfina in a heart-rending decision to allow her daughter to live with the Shimealls and get an education, Julia wrote:

Late October 1968
Dear Aaron and Hur,

Delfina and her younger brother Manuel are with me in Tetelcingo, in the state of Morelos. This is a small Aztec village where SIL has a house for rent by their members. It's some sixty miles south of Mexico City by a new freeway. Here, we enjoy running water that is pure enough not to boil. We have electricity, so we can use our electrical appliances and, incidentally, an electric typewriter which was a loving gift from friends in Oregon. So this letter is from a pioneer missionary going soft in her old age!

Panchita is still with us. The last legal step was the American Embassy in Mexico City where we caused no small stir. They had never had a case like hers. (Incidentally, we would like to reassure you that Panchita is *not* being adopted. The Shimealls are guardians, no more. She fully belongs to her Mommy.)

The outcome was that her name was placed on a long list of people who are waiting for immigration to the United States. When her turn comes, she will be permitted to go. But for now she is in school. The class consists of her and another little girl. Her teacher is Joyce Brewer, the daughter of missionaries who is spending a year with her parents before going on to college. Every school day for Panchita is a sheer delight in learning. She is the type of child with that special disposition that seems to always take things by the right handle. We love her!

Months later, after Panchita's passport had been approved and she was comfortably settled in her new home with the Shimealls, Julia added this to her late November 1969 letter.

Dear Aaron and Hur,

Tapes come from Little Braveheart: "Don't worry Mommy, I am fine. Every day I learn something. We studied about the moon today." Summer was filled with swimming and camping, living on a Florida beach and learning to ride a bicycle. Now the mails bring us school papers.

"Some good and some not so good," she freely admits. There are Brownies and dental appointments and a "pregnant white rat." But as are the loving mercies of our God, there have been overweights of joy.

Sincerely, in our mighty Lord of Hosts, *Julia*

To read Julia's letters is to realize that they are an ongoing journal chronicling the events of her everyday life that she considered significant to record. In addition, Julia often included philosophic comments at the end of her letters that put a positive spin on any negative experiences she had related. In an "Early March 1970," letter, Julia had this to say about how, just ten miles from reaching their destination of Comitán, her car was struck by a truck.

The impact from the crash threw us a hairsbreadth from two youngsters, one of whom escaped with a bruised leg. This was a devastating experience. We felt as if the fury of hell had been unleashed on us. That suddenly we were the chief actors in that age-long play, *The struggle between Good and Evil.* The outcome of that story would have been very different had the boys been killed. In all probabilities, we could no longer consider it reasonable or possible to live and work in that part of the country. As it was, there was only considerable damage to the car coupled with the harassment of extensive car repairs over an anxious period of months.

From what happened next to Julia, her March letter might more appropriately have read, "Beware the Ides of March." One day, after returning to Mexico City, Julia stepped out of her office for a ten-minute break. When she returned, the wallet in her purse, which had a considerable amount of money, was, as she said, "lifted." To add insult to injury, she related how a few months before her car was broken into and everything was "cleaned out." At the end of that paragraph, Julia said simply:

> God still has unexpected ways and means of reminding us that we are not to be materialistically minded.

A car break-in, accident and theft of money from her very limited budget were compounded by a series of illnesses that both she and Delfina battled. And then came a letter from her sister saying she hadn't understood a word she was trying to say in one of her letters. Whereupon Julia wrote:

> I was just trying to say I was bone-weary with one bothersome thing after another. Just this morning I had a ladder collapse under me resulting in a painful (and humiliating) fall on a cement floor, with various appendages draped around the rungs. So I keep flipping back to Job 1. There I've rediscovered the refrain which continues echoing down through the ages of God's dealing with those whom He loves and disciplines. And while he was yet speaking, there

came another...and another...and another....
Calamity on Calamity, for it was Job whom God
chose as our great forerunner in godly patience
under severe trial. But the chapter ends in
triumph. "Naked came I out of my mother's
womb and naked shall I return thither. The Lord
gave and the Lord hath taken away; blessed be
the name of the Lord! In all this Job sinned not,
nor charged God foolishly." In comparison to
Job, my trials seem so trivial I hesitate to
mention them. But to each trial he comforts. We
are finding those very ancient words in the most
ancient of books as a cooling wind upon our
troubled spirits. So we take courage.

Sincerely, in our mighty Lord of Hosts, *Julia*

10

Wearing Three Hats

One thing was clear, Julia loved life. She believed God had called her first to himself, and then to a specific purpose in his Kingdom as a Bible translator. Thus, no matter the perplexities, uncertainties and ambiguities on the world stage, Julia accepted life psychologically, believing God was in control. This was never more clearly demonstrated in her January 1975 letter.

> Dear Aaron and Hur,
>
> This is a brand-new year and today is one of those rare days in this large city [Mexico City]. A crisp wind is blowing and has lifted the thick mantle of man-made pollution. From the window where I write, our beautiful Sleeping Lady mountain has burst into sight in all of her new-fallen snow splendors. She speaks a private parable to me. "You see I am here. Many times you can't see me. The murk and filth of man's

making obscures me. However, I am here, always here. Take heart my child."

What joy it is to enter a New Year with Him who from everlasting to everlasting is God. Inflation is a change of values. God never changes. Recession? God still owns the cattle on a thousand hills. The changing morality? We trust in the great I AM that I AM. Insecurity? Underneath are his everlasting arms. Old age? "But Thou art the same and Thy years shall have no end." Biafra, Bangladesh, India, typhoons, cyclones, world population? Into Thy hands, O God, we commit the evils of this world. Our trust in thee includes the Trust of the Unexplained. In the whirr and stir of all these disturbances, make me an instrument of Thy peace. Hallelujah, what a Savior!

Throughout her many years of service with Wycliffe, Julia was a faithful correspondent, as witnessed by the chronology of her letters that make up the basis of these chapters. However, there is an gap of five years between 1970 (the conclusion of chapter nine) and 1975 (the beginning of this chapter) in which only a few letters survive. What is curious about these "silent" years is that in 1972 the long-awaited Tojolabal New Testament was published. Yet there remains almost nothing of Julia's lyrical writing style to commemorate this significant achievement.

Fortunately, there are bits and pieces from the Mexico Branch Director's reports that give us clues to why Julia may not have written much during this period. One reason may have been because for a year she was assigned to group secretarial service in the SIL headquarters in Mexico City. Another was that she became seriously ill in 1973 with an unknown illness and underwent emergency surgery. However, to celebrate the Mexico Branch's one hundredth published New Testament, Marianna Slocum (translator of two Tzeltal New Testaments) wrote a short bio about Julia and the Tojolabal work that fills in some of the blanks.

When the Tojolabal New Testament was ready for publication in 1972, there were perhaps a dozen believing households. At that time, we felt an order of 2000 copies was far too optimistic. Only a handful was literate, and persecution had scattered the first group of believers. Some had ventured into the jungles where they hoped to homestead and make a new beginning. Others had settled in the town of Las Margaritas where they attended church services in Spanish.

In 1972, Julia Supple with her co-worker Mary Mast returned to Las Margaritas with the newly printed Tojolabal New Testament. One of the several groups of Tojolabals who came to meet Julia was a new group of believers from the small town of Benito Juárez. They had been reached by Mexican Christians but were eager to have the Tojolabal New Testament and invited Julia and Mary to come and teach them to read.

On the eve of that trip to Benito Juárez, Julia did write about how excited she was to be taking the Tojolabal New Testament to the people of that village. Yet at age fifty-three she expressed some misgivings about her physical strength and ability to pioneer in primitive surroundings.

For this beautiful gift of the Tojolabal New Testament we thank our God, who made it all possible. Yet, I am experiencing the fear of the unknown. I wonder what the jungle country will be like? Will I be able to cope happily with primitive living conditions? Will I stay healthy? Like separate small scrolls, I roll out each fear before the Lord, who is telling me, *Bless the Lord, O my soul and forget not all his benefits. He will satisfy thy desire with good things so that thy youth is renewed like the eagle.* And each fear disappears as the dew with the rising of the morning sun.

At the conclusion of that letter, Julia wrote:

And do not forget to pray for me, I'm an extremely weak Christian sent to accomplish a great big impossible task. So you can easily conclude who has to do the job.

The Joy of the Lord is my strength, *Julia*

Six months later in June 1972 Julia sent her praying partners the following report.

Dear Aaron and Hur,

Benito Juárez, you wouldn't believe it! Located in the Eyseba River Valley, the village consists of some fifty thatched-roofed huts tucked away in the lush green verdant jungle country. To the northeast, there is a towering mountain range but these agile bodied Indians did not hesitate to scale these steep mountains to get word down to the other side that we had arrived. And people have poured in ever since our arrival.

That was June 4. Since we arrived, we have been received into this small part of the family of God with open arms. We are continually surrounded by our new loving friends. I've been patted, rubbed and stroked. Even my feet are objects of their tender loving care. It isn't the most fun thing that's ever happened to me. But after my survival training at Jungle Camp, I know I can handle anything.

Mary and I fill our days with teaching school, attending services, entertaining visitors and coping with semi-primitive living conditions. Mary helps in the clinic. The Christians built us a small palm leaf roofed hut. Beds are rough hewn boards elevated above a dirt floor. My security blanket is a cheesecloth mosquito net that keeps out large ferocious looking rats down to small pesky flying insects. I then tuck myself in for a bit of coveted privacy and escape from being public property.

God has done a beautiful work in this place. The man who pioneered this village took his machete and literally carved out a place to live for himself and his family. But when his family began to have serious health issues, he crossed over the mountains to get medical help from the Christian Tzeltals [in Corralito]. It was there that Gregorio first heard of God's love for him. So fascinated was he with the Christian story that he stayed in Corralito for nine months. Afterward, as a new believer in Jesus Christ, Gregorio brought the good news of the gospel back to Benito Juárez. There is now a small chapel that fills up for services.

There is also a small clinic staffed by a young Tzeltal man who functions as a medic.[21] His name is Alberto and even though his Tojolabal is halting, he has done a fine job of nurturing the

---

21 The translation team of Marianna Slocum and nurse Florence Gerdel produced two Tzeltal New Testaments, one for the highland and one for the lowland Tzeltal. In addition, Florence developed a fine clinic at Corralito that handled about seventy out-patients a day. Along with treating individual patients, Florence wrote a series of medical handbooks in Tzeltal and trained and sent out thirty-five young men as paramedicals. Each had received on-the-job training as both clinic workers and Bible teachers. Alberto Gomez was one of these paramedical evangelistic Bible teachers. Under his leadership, the men of Benito Juárez built an adequate airstrip at the edge of the village that made it possible to keep him supplied with medicines.

young Tojolabal congregation and treating the sick and injured. However, it now seems important to the Tojolabal church that since there are a number of literate Christians, they should be the ones to teach and lead their own people. Mary and I continue with our literacy class and are encouraged with the progress of the students. Lord willing, I plan to be in Phoenix and California during the last three months of the year.

Sincerely in Christ, *Julia*

****

If there ever were days of innocence in American culture, the late sixties and seventies shattered all such notions. The lexicon filled with new words, such as *Watergate, Human Rights, Feminism, The Cultural Revolution, Vietnam* and *Racism*, that captured people's imagination and changed the order of Western life forever. In late July 1976, writing from Las Margaritas, Julia, while absorbed in the new developments of the Tojolabal work, wanted to inform her constituents that she was aware of these many earth-shaking events.

Dear Aaron and Hur,

Chili beans simmer on the stove as I sit out in the yard absorbing the sunshine. Here in the middle of the rainy season the days are cool. Surrounded by all shades of lush greens and breathing clean and transparent air, we find ourselves exhilarated in a sparkling world.

For the past six weeks, I have been bent over a tape recorder putting the words of the New Tojolabal New Testament on tape, this in anticipation of the church in Benito Juárez using the tapes for their once-a-week fifteen-minute radio program, "The Tojolabal Hour." Mary and her two language helpers are working on a Tojolabal dictionary. We both come to the end of the day feeling fatigued, but it's a satisfying fatigue. It's nice to have that "Lord; I've done my best for You today" feeling.

If I convey to you that we are totally absorbed in this work, completely cut off from the bicentennial year or the horrible conflict in Lebanon, or the election in Italy or the struggle of the African nations or the drama of Entebbe, well, we're not. My prayer is:

Lord, teach us to apply our hearts to wisdom in this passing world scene. Help us to be sensitive and aware, but, at the same time, consumed with the desire to be wholly your people, loving and serving our own generation. Give us an untroubled spirit. Make us Your optimists, with a free and joyful heart. Grant us always to remember that the Lord reigneth now and forever more.

Julia ended her letter with a note that "a good number of Tojolabal young people were becoming more and more aware about the "outside world" and were struggling to emerge and be a part of the cultural sea change.

Many of the young people are hindered from moving forward by a lack of schooling, and often from their family who don't want their sons to move away. It is terribly frustrating and often depressing for them. Some of these are Christian young people. I ask you to pray for them. They are plagued by the usual confusion of minority groups both from within and without. Pray for the least painful transition possible.

Julia

In January 1977, Julia wrote an ecstatic letter about how fascinating it was to be discovering new Tojolabal words and phrases.

Dear Aaron and Hur,

One of the most fascinating facets of my life has been the Tojolabal language. For over a month, Antonia, a teenager fresh out of her village, has been teaching me "teen-age talk." As a result, I've collected a good-sized stack of new words for our dictionary file. It is a delight to me to be continually making linguistic discoveries, even if it's only a single word.

And this to me is a metaphor for *the truth*. However long our earthly sojourn, we will always be discovering the ways of God. Perhaps this is my prime New Year's wish for you and me—to be so childlike that we may experience the wonder of finding out more and more about Him. And there will never be enough years or time, that's why eternity is such a good idea.

As ecstatic as Julia was at the beginning of her January letter, her concluding paragraph was more somber. She hinted that her future among the Tojolabals was uncertain. However, Julia gave no details beyond saying that she was expecting to be in Southern California to have some minor surgery sometime after April. Then as she had done in so many of her letters, she gave a benediction for herself and her praying partners and friends.

My spiritual aspirations for the years are that they be backed by the intense desire that the whole of our lives be towards the accomplishment of what we are asking from God. Never give in, never be discouraged, that prayer is not only to God but with God. And that with God, all things are possible.

A ten o'clock scholar, *Julia*

To the surprise of most of her friends, Julia's next letter was dated late October 1977 and postmarked Garden Grove, California. In many ways, the letter is a puzzlement. We learn only by inference that Panchita[22] was with her for the summer. And then, without any explanation, we find

---

[22] Panchita, the daughter of Delfina, came to the States in 1967 for her schooling. Dick and Joan Shimeall became her legal guardians. See Chapter Nine for more details.

Julia and Panchita standing on a hill overlooking the pretty Mexican town of Las Margaritas with its stone fences and profusion of flowers weeping and saying goodbye to the town and their many friends as they plan to spend an extended time in Southern California. At first, we do not know exactly why Julia has suddenly made the decision to leave Mexico.

Dear Aaron and Hur,

In late August 1977, when we arrived in Southern California, it fell on me to look for housing. School would start in a week for Panchita, now a junior in High School, and she needed to be settled. After looking at some slummy unfurnished apartments for $195.00 a month, I went into culture shock. It was all I could do to keep turning tail and head back to our nine-room fifteen dollar [a month] abode in Southern Mexico. How *mad* can Californians get? Their economy is absolutely maniacal!

This whole change of plans was so sudden and so disrupting. In my wildest imagination, I never thought God would ask me to come to the U.S. with Panchita. You remember her don't you? She was that fairy-like miniature person with sparkly dark eyes who was about six years old when you saw her. She's been in the U.S. for nine years [under the guardianship of Dick and Joan Shimeal] and now needs some special attention. And I am now treading in where angels fear to tread.

We are now settled in a pleasantly furnished, two-bedroom apartment in a middle-class neighborhood. On my way here I kept reminding God that a teenager needs a private bedroom. At the time, I had no idea that it costs more money to rent a two-bedroom apartment. Such is my negative. However, God loves to give us what we ask for.

So now Panchita is in school. She works two hours in the afternoon at the District School Office. I commute daily from Garden Grove to Wycliffe's US corporate office in Huntington Beach.[23] It's there that I contribute a small part in Wycliffe's editorial department.

My finances are on the same basis as they were in Mexico. I am not subsidized. None of our Wycliffe workers are. It's the same-old story of God supplying every single need, now only it's two people instead of one. How naughty it would be to doubt Him at this point. In fact, it would be just plain sinful.

Mary (my co-worker) stays on in Mexico plugging away at the Tojolabal dictionary. As for me, my plans are indefinite as I endeavor to

---

[23] In 1999, this office was relocated to Orlando, Florida.

understand His wishes for me to stay or move on. However, it seems right that I stand by Panchita at least for this school year. So in my next letter to you, I'll make an attempt to share my feelings about living with a teenager. It's maddening. It's hilarious. It's creative, and it's destroying. I know you've been through it all. But remember this is happening to an old maid who could be her grandma.

After three months of "learning to be a parent to a modern teenager," Julia acknowledged that while it was hard to cope with Rock music, peer-pressure, and appropriate dress, "things were looking up." She said she felt better today than she did yesterday, and she felt better yesterday than the day before that. One reason for this new optimism was her editorial and writing responsibilities at the Wycliffe office.

Dear Aaron and Hur,

The job at the office is the joy of my life. I love going to work every day. I'm writing radio scripts that are aired in different parts of the country. This involves research and background studies of our Wycliffe workers from all over the world. It's great fun.

And Panchita's enjoying her office job as well. She works two hours each day during the school week. Her first check was for $25.00, I told her I used to work eight hours five days a week for $17.00! She was impressed.

Now a bit of this-n-that. Panchita and I live in an apartment complex in Garden Grove. It's eight miles to the office in Huntington Beach. My faithful nine-year-old VW bug has been my transport back and forth. But I came by bus one morning. This will save some money. I have to walk about five blocks from the bus stop to the office, but this is good for me. I hear from the grapevine that I am going to become the manager of the apartments. This involves collecting rents, telling people to turn down their TV, calling the police when there are fights, picking up suicides, watering the lawn and a few other miscellaneous duties. So this will be my third hat to wear. Radio Script Writer, Apartment Manager, Mother, but the greatest is MOTHER. I hope you pray for me.

I love you all very much, *Julia*

11

Plunking the First String

To be sure, Romans 8:28 (NLT) *"And we know that God causes everything to work together for the good of those who love God,"* is a paradox for many believing Christians who are not pleased with their lives. Yet, the overwhelming testimony of mature Christians is that God does indeed intermingle all things for good in their lives. Their experience is that the events they once believed were disastrous and bitterly disappointing worked out for good and their greater blessing.

When Julia left Mexico and assumed the responsibility for Panchita's schooling and care, it was with the painful reality that she might never again return to Mexico and work among the Tojolabal people. However, within a few months after her decision and willingness to relocate and trust God to work out His plan for her, she was to enjoy a period of unexpected sweetness that far exceeded her wildest dreams. In March of 1978, she wrote about it.

Dear Aaron and Hur,

For thirty-five years, I have been plunking away
pretty much on one string: Bible translation, or
Wycliffe, or the Tojolabal people, whatever. And
I am still plunking, but now it's a bit different.
I'm not actually *doing* those things, but I am
writing about them. That's the way it should be,
of course, because you can't really write about
something until you've experienced it.

Now I am plunking away on another string. It's
called *Israel.* Let me tell you how it happened. A
long time ago a dear friend sent me a thousand
dollars earmarked for a trip to Israel. When I
received the gift, life was then too demanding. I
was too busy plunking the first string. And then
last month I did it. I went to Israel.

Curiously, Julia's love affair with Israel did not include
most of the typical tourist sites, such as the Church of the
Nativity. They were, in her eyes, "too commercialized and
somewhat vulgar." The jewel that dazzled her was Lake
Galilee. She offered that it was "still there" and said an
afternoon sailing across its historic waters was "pretty
exciting." The upper Galileen countryside impressed her, as
did Mt. Zion and the Mt. of Olives. And then, she wrote,
"There was Jerusalem, a city like no other anywhere." With
a feeling of spiritual compatibility, Julia also entered into
the lives of the Jewish people she met along the way. As
she continued her letter:

After meeting and talking to Prime Minister
Menachem Begin, we enjoyed the hospitality of a
Jewish couple from Brooklyn, who are now
Israeli citizens. I'll never forget that evening. I
stood in the trenches on the Golan Heights on
the exact spot where 250 brave Israeli soldiers
laid down their lives to pay for those hills. For
three memorable nights, we slept in a kibbutz
near the Lebanon border and heard the sporadic
burst of machine-gun fire from those who were
unhappy with the Israelis' presence in the area.
But there was a kind of electric feeling in the
atmosphere. And when they danced and sang for
us, as only the Israelis can, I felt the tremendous
courage of these people of the land. It's
impossible to explain the emotions that surged
through me as I recalled the Psalm: *By the rivers of
Babylon, there we sat down, yea, we wept, when we
remembered Zion. We hanged our harps upon the willows
in the midst thereof. For there they that carried us away
captive required of us a song; and . . . mirth, saying, Sing
us one of the songs of Zion. How shall we sing the Lord's
song in a strange land?* (137:1-4, KJV).

But that evening I was the only one weeping in
joy for them. They are no longer in a strange
land. Talk about emotions! I had to fasten my
seat belt, or I'd have gone straight into orbit. It's
really true. The land does something to you. I
couldn't have stayed on that high for much

longer. However, getting back home with a high school teenager in tow was the perfect antidote. I am earth bound again.

Julia

By June of 1978, the euphoria of Julia's trip to Israel had all but evaporated and given way to the concrete reality of daily living. There was still her eight-mile commute to Huntington Beach and radio scripts to be written. To sharpen her writing skills, she spent a week at Biola College (now University) in a writers' workshop. She was also involved with Toastmasters, which she thought would give her increased confidence in speaking about Wycliffe's work. And, of course, there was Panchita, who, said Julia, was a "very nice person to live with." Julia then admitted that most of the disharmony in the home started with her. This usually came from probing for more information than Panchita wanted to divulge. Or perhaps it was Julia becoming disgruntled over a messy room.

All this was in her June letter, including the anticipated date for Panchita's graduation from high school, after which, Julia speculated, she would return to Mexico for perhaps another three or four years. Then in late August Julia wrote about Panchita's terrible mishap. Departing from her standard salutation she began with:

Dear Un-Aaron and Un-Hur,

The "Un" is because this letter won't be going to the Aaron and Hur list of people but just to you folks who've written or sent money. It's my new sixty's way of writing letters. Now I know you probably don't approve 100% of this method. You would rather have something scribbled in my own handwriting that is a bit more personal. Actually, I agree. The problem is I don't get those short notes written. So this is my "Un" letter to you.

Now let me share my heart. A few weeks ago on July 13th, life was going along as usual. I was having an afternoon stretch-out when Panchita came home with her friend Debbie and said she would walk her home. I said, "Okay, fine with me." But the next thing was a phone call from Debbie, who said they'd be coming right away with Panchita, and I should take her immediately to the hospital! Debbie said Panchita had fallen and split her chin open and knocked out her teeth. And what a split chin it was! It looked like raw meat hanging there. So off we went to the hospital. Three hours, several x-rays and a sewed-up-chin later we came back home. No fractured skull or jaw. Now we had time to reflect.

It was one of those freakish accidents that often happen when young people decide to race each other. When Debbie challenged Panchita to see who could reach her home first, Panchita slipped and fell flat on her chin on the pavement. And to add insult to injury, Debbie also fell, not on the pavement but, *clonk*, right on top of Panchita's head.

The result was that her back molars broke into dozens of pieces.

What followed was a month-long series of oral surgeries and extensive dental work that included gold capping and permanent bridges for the teeth that couldn't be saved. Julia noted that even after a month Panchita still didn't have full use of her tongue. For those who wondered how Julia would pay for such expensive dental work, she thanked God for insurance, not hers, but the Shimeall's.

> If you are wondering how in the world I would ever pay for such dental catastrophe, I am pleased to tell you, and praise the Lord, that Panchita is under eighteen and, therefore, is covered by the Shimeall's family insurance which will cover eighty percent of the cost. (The Shimealls are still her legal guardians.) Even the twenty percent would wipe me out. I am pleased to tell you that the Lord has given us a small amount to help on the costs, and the Shimeall's are assuming the remaining costs. That, too, is overwhelming.

> And not to be undone with blessing, I received a phone call from Panchita's mom telling me she was on her way to be with Panchita. What is amazing about this is we had not notified Delfina about the accident, but we believe God just sent her. And for the entire month that Panchita was pretty puny and hollowed eyed she had her real mommy to pamper her and be with

her while I kept on working. I haven't missed a beat. Panchita is the one who missed the beat. This is almost a pun, since she had a summer job at the Garden Grove Police Department. And she could have used the money.

In addition to writing radio scripts, Julia was also asked to write feature articles and profile pieces for *In Other Words*, Wycliffe's then publicity magazine. In the October 1978 issue of *In Other Words,* Julia answered a much-asked question about singleness. In response to a woman named Ruth, Julia wrote the following article called *Singleness of Heart*:

Dear Ruth:

I have been asked to answer your letter of inquiry regarding single missionaries, their troubles and triumphs. If experience has qualified me for this article, I should be an expert on the subject.

Let me clear the decks by saying I am not akin to those who deny they would like to have been married, to have had the love and security and normalcy of family life on the mission field. That is right and good. I'm wary of the singles who sputter a lot. I suspicion a façade or guilt feelings for not having fulfilled the accepted role in society and life in general.

Here is my basic spiritual and philosophic position on this interesting subject. It is neither better to be married nor to be single. These are only facts of life. What really matters are our acceptance and reaction to whatever state in which we find ourselves. I believe this is borne out by the Holy Scriptures.

Assuming that we as individuals have followed on to know the Lord, having established a life pattern of continually walking in the light we believe God gives us, I see no reason under heaven or on earth to be unhappy or frustrated. And I do not believe the marrieds have a corner on creativity. Have you ever painted a picture, written a poem, or decorated a room, made a dress, translated a New Testament, planted a tree, or led someone to love Jesus Christ? Not one thing is exactly like another but tremendously exciting and satisfying and creative. God made us to be creative, all of us.

There will always be false assumptions floating around such as: All single people are frustrated. And that is true! The error lies in the conclusion that only single people are frustrated. So, as occasion arises, I quietly correct that assumption. No one has a corner on frustration. It's a commonly shared people-problem. And it is no more fair to conclude that a single person's frustration is because of their singleness than to say that a married person's is because he or she is married.

Let's consider the single missionary with strong romantic notions—a product of conditioning that produces dreams of a perfect mate, a marriage made in heaven. She makes a project of landing a husband. Then to her dismay, she awakens to the fact that the knight in white armor is not riding around in the backwoods. The present ratio in Wycliffe is 660 single women to 88 single men. And those are statistics with a thud! I would venture that most of us women, however, have our reckless moments when we feel if we were in the right place at the right time, we could land one of those 88. But that keeps the old spark in the eye and chins up.

However, unharnessed dreams and imaginations, not brought into the captivity of Christ, have resulted in tragedy. Numbers of God's missionaries have settled for far less than their noble dreams. Their holy call has come into dispute, and some mission boards have panicked. The result? Refusal of single missionaries. But this seems to me a very harsh measure and the resultant denial to a dying world of thousands of dedicated lives, which can be poured out into loving service. I believe mission boards must take risks because no war was ever won without a risk. Just because of a few tragedies, we should not throw out the baby with the bath water.

Further, I oppose a rigid classification of married people and single people. A balanced life with a holy purpose must include everyone. It will love children and old people, married people and singles. The very nature of a mission organization brings people together and intertwines their lives in a common cause of love and service to Christ. I love and appreciate Wycliffe's marrieds and feel my love and appreciation are reciprocated. I have occasion now and then to remind one of them that being single does not particularly equate unhappiness.

Let me sum this up. Happiness is not the goal of life. Doing the will of God, walking in obedience to God's Spirit and living a life of creativity in God, that's the kind of stuff that brings satisfaction and joy to anyone. It matters not one whit what happens, but it matters tremendously how we accept it. I might add that I have not achieved this high calling, but I press ever onward. If you are hesitant about mission service because you are single, I hope this encourages you to give back to Christ's loving heart and let Him channel that love where it is so needed.

Very sincerely in Christ, *Julia Supple*

Julia's letter was a true expression of how she felt about her own singleness and mission career. And I expect it also reflected the attitude of most of the single women in

Wycliffe at that time, and even to the present. Although believing it necessary to be actively engaged in the work where the Lord had placed them, most single women also kept an open mind to what God might have for them in the future.

As for Julia, her immediate future was about to take on a new and totally unexpected shift of focus that was to add a new richness to her life. As she wrote her 1978 Thanksgiving-Christmas letter, Julia only hinted at this new event by saying:

> The months ahead will be eventful. Panchita turns 18 on December 5, and my Day is February 14. I will send you all a very special letter for that one.

But that was all the information she gave. Except that, while she was composing her thoughts and writing her letter, she was toying with a gold chain around her neck on which hung a ring with two perfectly beautiful diamonds set side by side. It was her engagement ring.

12

It's Good To Be Married

In 1940, twenty-eight-year old Lloyd (Andy) Andrus
proposed marriage to a young twenty-one-year-old Julia
Helen Supple. At first, Julia agreed to become Mrs. Lloyd
Andrus, but then, with regret, said "no" to the proposal.
Her reason? She felt an overwhelming compulsion that
God was calling her to work as a cross-cultural Bible
translation missionary in Mexico. This was to be her first
allegiance.

Andy and Julia went their separate ways, he to fight his
country's battles in the Pacific theater of World War II,
Julia to work among the Tojolabal people of Southern
Mexico. When the war was over, Andy settled in Phoenix,
Arizona, married, raised three children, worked as an
accountant, and served in his local church. Over the years,
Julia would speak and give a report at Morningside
Presbyterian in Phoenix.

Several years after Andy's wife died, he and Julia
reconnected. And here I speculate about the details. There
is no written record and few of her friends or colleagues

who worked with Julia in the then Wycliffe headquarters in Huntington Beach recall exactly how she and Andy got back together. One of her colleagues suggested that Andy may have visited Morningside Presbyterian Church to hear Julia speak or give a report. One of Julia's colleagues, Valarie Stevenson, did note that when she and Andy met, "sparks began to fly." Valarie also explained that theirs was a long-distance phone romance between Garden Grove, California and Phoenix, Arizona. Julia herself once remarked how large her phone bill had become.

Then sometime in October of 1978, Julia showed her colleagues a diamond ring she wore around her neck. She told them how Andy Andrus had first asked her to marry him in 1940 and that he had now, in 1978, asked her once again. This time Julia said "yes" and to commemorate this happy event, Andy had selected two beautiful diamonds to represent the first and second time he had asked for her hand in marriage.

The reason for the secrecy about her engagement had to do with a Wycliffe rule that required dismissal from the organization for any Wycliffe member who became engaged to marry a non-Wycliffe person. In Julia's case, however, Andy had applied to become a Short Term Assistant (STA), which meant that Andy, after going through a vetting process, would be considered a legitimate Wycliffe member. In October, Andy was just in the process of applying for STA status and thus Julia did yet not want to announce her official engagement. In fact, there is some interesting correspondence between the then director of the Mexico branch, John Alsop, and Julia. He wanted her to return to Mexico and complete the Tojolabal dictionary, to which Julia made this reply:

Dear John,

I hate to disagree with your strong directive for Lloyd and me to return to the Tojolabal work. At the moment, I feel I am in the place as a writer where I am the most productive. Also, Lloyd is seven years older than I am, and it seems foolish to start such a staggering project as a Tojolabal grammar and dictionary and for Lloyd to live in a strange new country. Having said this, I have to say that this is my idea, not Lloyd's. Also, I agree this is a fine and worthy project, and I suggest that the Platteels[24] consider this as one of their projects. They would learn a great deal about the language. I realize we can't tell them what to do. But we might encourage them. They are really sharp at language learning.

The reason why all this must be on the hush is timing. I'm not supposed to be officially engaged at this time until Lloyd becomes an STA (legally). If the group administration knew I was

---

[24] Henny and Chris Platteel were assigned by The Reformed Church of America to work in partnership with SIL among the Tojolabal people. (See more in the Afterword about the Platteel's, Sam and Helen Hofman, and Brian and Donna Renes, also later assigned to work among the Tojolabal.)

officially engaged I could be kicked out of the organization. I plan a February 14th announcement at the Huntington Beach office when by that time Lloyd should have his full-fledged STA membership. I repeat it seems best for us to remain here in the US as members of the US Division. I can continue on writing radio scripts, a job I love, and Lloyd can work in the finance department. Having said this, I do want to do what is right. I know I almost promised to do that dictionary. But at this point, given Lloyd's age, I don't think I should get involved in such a stressful long-term project.

Thank you for bearing with me and forgiving me, which you must do, of course. I really didn't plan all this, it's just one of those goodies the Lord let come my way. Take it from me, you can be just as excited about a good man at sixty as you can at twenty!

God bless, *Julia*

Julia's official engagement announcement was planned for her birthday, February 14, and she planned to be married in early March 1979. But her March letter to "Aaron and Hur," told a revised story.

Dear Aaron and Hur,

I had never heard of it before, and none of my friends had. So I must be the only bride in history who married with a full-blown case of pink eye! Happily, I had some very chic dark glasses. Then, in the home of Ken and Vivian Watters, with nine understanding friends supporting us, we took our vows and I became Mrs. Lloyd (Andy) Andrus on February 6, 1979. I'm amazed how the few words we repeated made life suddenly become…well, different! Just months ago I recycled an old article on singlemess. It was published in, *In Other Words.* Shortly after that, Lloyd proposed again. That "again" is because he'd first proposed in 1940. Though my answer was then affirmative, I soon reneged and went to Mexico and he, to the sands of Iwo Jima to help fight that vicious war. We got together after a Tojolabal New Testament, for me, and for him, three lovely children and five "grands." No woman is more appreciated and loved than I. And it's *so* special to belong and to be loved and cherished and tenderly cared for.

My association with Wycliffe is the same. I continue to be a full member. Lloyd is a Short Term Assistant. While I continue in the editorial department, he works in the Wycliffe Book Room sales promotion. And to expedite life, we live only a ten-minute drive from the office.

While she extolled the joys of nuptial bliss, Julia also, in splendid candor, revealed that two people of a certain age and different temperaments require an adjustment of their normal *modus operandi.*

When two people our age marry, move and pool their life collection of things, it takes time to reorganize and recapture any semblance of an orderly lifestyle. Our mobile home is beginning to resemble a place where two sane people dwell. For days, we lived in an unreal world where finding anything turned into a major search. It inevitably ended up by *my* becoming the guilty culprit. The result, of course, of my husband's having been an orderly accountant and my having been a creative writer.

Take lost stamps, for instance. They just disappeared. For days all searching was in vain. Lloyd's solution? To locate them, of course! And mine? Buy more—why flay our emotions unnecessarily? So we compromised. We bought a *few* stamps. Shortly afterwards I found the lost ones in a perfectly logical place, the desk drawer. But who expects to find stamps in logical places? So I conclude that life will continue to be interesting with the union of a very organized man and a quasi-organized woman. Lloyd's amazed that I've reached sixty intact.

Well so much for the zany part of life. It's good to be married, to have a home and a man to love. It's good to belong to Wycliffe. And with a typewriter at the end of my fingers, it's good to share the gorgeous story of God's great power and love to thousands who listen to our "Translation Report" by radio. It's even good to be sixty. I'm not afraid of tomorrow for I have seen yesterday, and I love today.

Sincerely, in Christ, *Julia Supple Andrus*

Six months after their wedding, Julia returned to Las Margaritas with Andy to "close up shop" and dispose of her household items, things like a table, chairs, pots and pans, and other kitchen utensils. There were books and picture hangings and various kinds of bric-a-brac. At first, this was all a pragmatic, necessary, logical step in keeping with Julia's recent lifestyle change. As she surveyed the items that were to be sold, Julia took this process of downsizing as a teachable moment to tell herself how *things* mattered so little. Or did they?

August 1979
Dear Aaron and Hur,

I have a squirrel nature. Or could it be a fear of running out of something? And my many years of living in Mexico didn't help. We were always far from the source of supply, thus instead of buying just one of something, I'd by two or three, or even four. I ended up owning four pressure cookers that were scattered in three different locations. Not only was there an initial investment, but I was paying rent on nine rooms and two storage bins to house these precious possessions. So obviously something had to be done.

However, I never dreamed I'd have difficulty getting rid of bedroom furniture and kitchen appliances. We'd sell them, and that would be that. And we did, all in one fell swoop. And I didn't think anymore about it until the new owners asked if they could move the stuff out before we left. And suddenly I burst into tears, big wet blobby ones. At that moment, I knew every piece of furniture was woven into the experience of those more than thirty years. How many pots of beans have I cooked on that *stove* to serve my Tojolabal friends who sat at that small table in those *chairs!* How many language problems did we discuss? These weren't just *things,* they had the heartbeat of joy and sorrow shared with a people God gave me to love. So disposing of all the stuff and saying the goodbyes was painful. But that was the purpose of the trip, and so our mission was accomplished.

Julia ended her newsletter with several news briefs that included an update on Panchita. From an earlier letter, we learned that she had a boyfriend who at first wasn't a believer, but over time became an enthusiastic follower of the Lord. Panchita was now sharing an apartment with a girlfriend and working in an office. Panchita's mother had gotten a good job with the Mexican government, and

Panchita was a taking a month-long vacation to visit her mother in Mexico. Julia then ended her letter with news of the Platteel's:

> Chris and Henny Platteel, missionaries with the Reformed Church in America, are carrying on the work among the Tojolabals. They're loving village living and learning the language. We hear of new believers in different places. We continue working in the Wycliffe office, I in writing, and Andy in the bookroom. For the last several months, Wycliffe has entered a new language area every seven days, and a New Testament has been coming off the press every nine days. That's GOOD NEWS!
>
> Sincerely, in Christ,
> *Julia* for Andy and Julia Andrus

In her next letter, it was clear that the emotional investment she had felt for her Tojolabal home in Mexico had given way to the enjoyment she took in her new place, a (mobile) home at 19251 Brookhurst, Sp. 126, Huntington Beach, California:

> Dear Aaron and Hur,
>
> Andy and I are thankful for a peaceful home in the context of a world in hurricane. I keep the inside and Andy manicures the outside. It's a quiet place where truth and honesty and warmth and love can put on their slippers and be at

home. And we can be ourselves, knowing we're safe with one another and with God. And when we do blow it, there's forgiveness and acceptance of one another's humanity.

A year later, in February 1980, this is what she had to say in response to a person who asked her if she was happy:

Dear Aaron and Hur,

It's been a year now. And since I'm among the very few of your friends who married at sixty for the first time, I'll give you a little rundown on what it's like. Recently, a friend asked, "Are you happy Julia?" Even before I was married, I've always had reservations answering that question. Perhaps it's because I'm not the bubbly type. Or because I am not sure what's meant by happiness. So I ended up going down rabbit paths.

I'm not *unhappy*, I tell myself. I love my husband, I even *like* him. I enjoy our home. I like shopping and cooking for two. I like surprising him and buying him presents. He's fun to tease. And laugh with over Erma Brombeck.[25] I love his bringing me a fresh rose in the morning. And holding hands as we walk, or blowing kisses

---

[25] Erma Louise Bombeck, an American humorist, achieved great popularity for her newspaper columns that described suburban home life from the mid-1960s until the late 1990s.

across the room. It's also nice to have exchanged "my" for "ours" and to get angry at the government together. But occasionally there are rough spots. Nothing serious. It's just that I spout off like the Irish person I am, and Andy is quieter. Just doing our own thing as a human being. Jean, the person who asked the "are-you-happy" question, drew her own conclusions. "You're contented," she said. I like *contented*. It fits my personality.

****

In 1940, there were 37 Wycliffe translators working in eighteen ethnic languages of one country, Mexico. In 1942, Wycliffe founder Cameron Townsend and the Mexico branch set a prayerful goal of adding fifty new members. God answered that prayer and in July 1942, Julia Supple became one of those fifty new members. In 1980, thirty-eight years after Julia joined Wycliffe, the membership was over 2,000 and Wycliffe workers were in more than a dozen countries.

But, of course, the world of the 1980s was very different from the one Julia knew in 1942. A new kind of community—the "global electronic village"—had begun to emerge as the personal computer became an indispensable tool for business, industry and Bible translation. The 1980's was also a time of rising terrorism that included airplane hijackings, unrest in the Middle East and insurrection in Latin America. Such Third World unrest was to have unsettling and dramatic changes for Wycliffe's work in

Mexico. Executing prudent diplomatic skill, Julia informed her constituents about nationalistic pressure that was affecting her colleagues in Mexico.

February, 1980
Dear Aaron and Hur,

Maybe you've heard about Mexico. There are people there with clout who have an opposing philosophy of what really matters in life. They're committed people, dedicated. So for the present, the Mexican government has stopped issuing papers necessary for SIL to continue working in the country. This means that more than half of the Mexico branch members will be leaving throughout the next twelve months.[26] Thus far, older members, with permanent immigrant status, can remain in the country.

Try to imagine what it means to suddenly have to rethink and rearrange your life, and to leave the people you love and serve. Remorse, tears, frustration, sadness, anger, tension. Mix these with undulating faith: is this *really* the will of God? Shall I accept it lying down? Who is the good guy and the bad guy in this? What stance

---

[26] To accommodate this exodus of its members from Mexico, the Mexico branch of SIL purchased property in Catalina, Arizona, a community near Tucson, and built an administrative center. Also, some individual members acquired property in the vicinity to build their own homes.

shall I take to lend dignity and honor to the gospel of Jesus Christ? What shall I do next? Help, Lord, I'm sinking!

So this is a call to prayer. Not only for the Wycliffe folk on the move, but also for the people they leave behind. The ones who barely know Jesus Christ, or that don't know Him at all. Ask God that we'll be able to look *beyond* our complex present. God has a perfect solution when doors close. Thus, whatever happens, we can hold our heads high and give the shout of triumph, and know that lives rooted in God are never uprooted.

I finish this letter with euphoria. More and more, I feel the need to get caught up with God in His overall plans. His thoughts aren't limited to Mexico. They're for the entire world. Someday these dark pieces of the puzzle will fit into the whole. Then it will make sense. And all will be well. If the piece you're working on is dark, look up. Look up and *laugh* because there's Someone up there looking down and laughing,

Julia Supple Andrus

13

The End of the Journey

Thornton Wilder, author of *The Bridge of San Luis Rey* and other prize winning books and plays, once wrote:

All that we know about those we have loved and lost is that they would wish us to remember them with more intensified realization of their reality. What is essential does not die but clarifies. The highest tribute to the dead is not grief but gratitude.[27]

In 1991, with the onset of diabetes and other health aliments, Julia had a change of status from an Active Member of WBT and SIL to Health Leave. Then, in 1993, her status changed from Health Leave to Retirement. She was seventy-four. Yet, she was still an active letter writer and engaged in life, her health problems notwithstanding.

In December of that year, she wrote one of the most

---

[27] *CONTEXT*, December 2010, Part B Volume 42, Number 12, p. 7.

extraordinary letters of her long career. Rather than address it to Aaron and Hur, she simply said:

Dear friends, everywhere:

One of my after-Christmas rituals is to fill in a new calendar with birthdays of friends and family, then to note to-do's on certain days through the 12 months ahead. That means that for four days I've been floating ideas around in my head, recalling the goodness of the Lord on my private parcel of the land of the living.

"We hadn't planned this for our golden years," a new friend remarked as she walked her handsome husband down the hall of the Veteran's home in Mt. Vernon, Missouri. It was the Alzheimer's wing, and Andy is there also. None of us plan for such pain in life, neither the patient nor the family. It just happens.

Alzheimer's comes on quickly. Something unusual, perhaps unpleasant, takes place. It could be a flare-up in a relationship or, like it was for Andy, something as mundane as forgetting where he kept his underwear. He could no longer find the gas station where he'd bought gas for years. "Honey, you're really getting absent-minded," I'd tell him. "Well you just wait until you're eighty years old!" he'd snap back. And life would go on, not normally, but somehow.

Years before, Andy had developed a paranoia about any mail that was slightly torn or ruffled. Someone, he thought, was tampering with it. I thought he was odd and crotchety, but so what? I had my own passel of peculiarities, so who was I, the pot, to call the kettle black. This went on for a long time.

As the disease advanced, so did the frustrations and conflicts. At some point, I'd tell myself something's wrong here, but what? *This guy is getting to be a real dingbat,* I'd say to myself. Then I began assessing my emotional energy. The excuses and explanations I'd made for him weren't working now. I'd swing from irritation to anger to feeling positively furious. One lady, who attends our Alzheimer's support group, told me what a loving and cordial relationship she'd always had with her mother. "And now, she moaned, I'm angry at her ninety-eight percent of the time." I know how she felt.

Reasoning with Andy was a waste of time. In the hot summer months of 1992, he insisted on closing all the windows. In July, I secretly unplugged the cord on his electric blanket which he continued to use. Arguing only made him more determined. In protest, I finally moved to our extra bedroom where I raised every window and could get some sleep. Until he left for the Vet's home in February this year, he was bugged by the "empty bed syndrome." "It isn't right to have that extra bed in there," he'd say. "We ought to rent it out." As time progressed, his sleeping patterns became more complicated. Night was day and day was night. No matter what time he laid down to rest, when he arose, he would insist on having breakfast. One day I fed him oatmeal three times. You can't go wrong on oatmeal. It lowers cholesterol!

Family and societal relationships got all messed up in his thinking. He could retain the ones that went back a long time. He remembered his two brothers and a deceased sister but his own three children and their families were gone. His parents would dart in and out of his memory. For weeks, he would check on the dog across the street, yes it was still there every morning. In fact, it was a gas meter. This man, who'd always enjoyed an unusual memory and who'd made a living as an auditor, was no longer able to balance his checkbook.

I was exhausted but unable to commit him to professional care. My intention was to nurse him until the day of his death, to love him, treat him with dignity and provide him security. Then he began tearing up important papers, slept less and less, refused to bathe and treated people with hostility. Each new weird behavior added to my pent-up anxiety and frayed emotions. As I reviewed the years, I realize there was no starting point. It was so gradual, but unrelenting, and it was not going to get better.

In late January, we celebrated Andy's 82nd birthday. A month later his daughter Sylvia and her husband Tom went with me to leave him at the wonderful Veteran's facility thirty-three miles from our home. We left him bewildered, asking Tom why he was letting them do this to him. My pain was excruciating, and that pain hangs on. Even as I write I weep. I came back to an empty house, no longer home because the man who had loved me so deeply and faithfully was gone. All my past anger and frustration turned into a torrent of grief so intense that after almost nine months I can relive those agonizing hours as though they were yesterday. Sometimes I walk through these rooms bellowing like a cow that's had her calf removed.

But day by day living has become easier, and the weeping has assuaged. I now enjoy the uncomplicated happiness of life like lunching with a friend or watching children at play. I laugh at the Lockhorns and The Family Circus. I'm reading books again. And I have a dream, a resurrected dream. I dream of becoming a writer, of stringing words together so that someone somewhere might be helped and comforted in this personal agony.

I shared this writing dream with my prayer group, all of whom are younger than I. I asked that they pray that this old clunker of a typewriter, which so faithfully typed the Tojolabal New Testament those many years ago, might be replaced. That evening I came home with an almost new electronic one. Later, another sparkly young woman in the printing business offered a computer. Both of these mysterious machines are loans, on my desk, waiting to be learned. In this interim, I am gathering a handful of ideas and loving the dreams of grandeur of becoming a famous writer! Ah, what challenges ahead for an aged lady! But washing the dishes and carrying out the garbage and cleaning the toilet bowl put it in perspective. A few rejections slips will help, too.

Hey, this was supposed to be a Christmas letter about the goodness of our Lord. It's the ancient paradox, isn't it, to discover the Son of God walking about with us in our fiery furnaces. How many times this year I've found in my Bible the very words of comfort and sustenance I've needed so desperately. So maybe the Emmanuel word of Christmas is the one for me this year. GOD WITH US. He's been alongside all the days of my life.

Then in a Job-like soliloquy, Julia listed twelve pithy laments about her life. At first glance one would wonder if instead of being so faithful, as Julia so valiantly declared, God had been rather capricious.

—my Andy, as he's retreated into a labyrinth of mental illness. "Do you remember Jesus? I asked him one time. "You mean the Lord Jesus? How could I forget him?" he responded.

—when the refrigerator warmed and dripped and made a mess, demanding a quick fix.

—when our kitchen door awning, weighted with icicles, fell off.

—when the old Mercury's tires showed steel and demanded replacing, all four of them.

—our summer lawn required a weekly mowing and a neighbor asked to do it.

—when a stove element burned out.

—when the car's headliner needed replacing.

—when major repairs had to be made on our mobile, expensive ones.

—when we suffered two financial setbacks, one from an incompetent broker and another from a dishonest home repair man.

—when a molar broke off and had to be capped. My mouth is becoming a treasure trove.

—when a great sucking noise between here and the Vet's Home gobbles up a big hunk of my budget for Andy's care.

So Emanuel, GOD WITH US, is not ethereal or poetic. It is life and substance. It becomes palpable when I pay the rent, buy the groceries and fill the car's tank with gas. "Have you lacked anything?" No dear Jesus, not one thing! You, the great God of heaven, have walked alongside me all year long, praise your holy name!

And my prayer for you is that you experience a rebirth of the joy of our ever-present Emmanuel this Christmas time.

Enfolded by his love, *Julia*

There may have been other Christmas letters, but the one that appears to have been her last is dated "Advent 1996" and written from English Village Park, Nixa, Missouri. From the opening preamble of her letter we learn that this area (she was born in Kansas City, Missouri) held special memories of her early childhood and young adolescence. All this before she moved to Phoenix for high school. No longer does Julia address her letter to Aaron and Hur, but simply:

Dear People, I've Loved So Long,

Down the road south, about thirty miles from here, leans an old decaying house where I remember becoming a person. I was just a little tyke, maybe four years old, playing among the wild persimmon tree by a dancing brook. It was there I recall the preliminary stirrings of God in my heart. As I reveled in my childhood world, I thought God must be good to give us such a pretty world in which to live.

Somehow, somewhere my mother, whom I called "Mama," had come into possession of a large wooden box that once packaged an upright piano that was stationed at the back of our house. This was the perfect meeting place for me and my imaginary playmates. My favorite was Prudence. She and I shared delicious secrets, and we played together for hours. I was alone but never lonely because Prudence was a forever-friend.

My older sister Lela was doing her high school far on the other side of town and Mama, as a widow, worked two jobs—she made biscuits for the hotel in town, then drove to Branson to sell real estate. "Babysitting" was not in our vocabulary back then, but some days I stayed with ladies who fed me scrumptious homemade bread and butter and sugar sandwiches. Mama's cheerful presence filled my evenings and early-morning hours. [Lela boarded at her school.] I have no negative memories of those times. Mama had been recently widowed and raising two girls in a rural Ozark setting could not have come easily. But God in his tender mercies helped her to plant a carefree happy spirit in my young heart.

After a long absence from these ancient hills, including an earth-shaking encounter with Jesus Christ and a forty-year stint of missionary service among the Tojolabal people of southern Mexico, life came full circle when Andy and I moved back here again. Now I, too, am widowed, and again, I am with a forever friend whose name is Jesus.

Perhaps a part of aging is remembering what God has forgotten. We tell ourselves how foolish we were along the way. Remember old Jacob as he stood before the friendly Pharaoh? "The days of the years of my pilgrimage are a hundred and thirty years" he lamented. "Few and evil have the days of my life been." That is why I love Advent. It's the coming of quiet joy, the arrival of radiant light in our darkness, full forgiveness and quiet comfort.

To those who have asked, I feel well (I'm seventy-seven), no aches or pains, though my energy level keeps lowering. I keep warm in winter and cool in summer. A new car this year takes me where I want to go. I still drive. A host of good people surround my life. I read good books and listen to good music. In my church, I'm the recipient of undeserving and lavish love. Under the anointed teaching, I'm learning more and more of the height and depth, width and length of God's love for us imperfect people.

For the next five years, Julia lived at 50 English Village Park, Nixa, Missouri. Then on August 14, 2001 at age eight-two, Julia wrote a hand-written note to her only niece, Claudia Cowan, with a new phone number and change of address:

> Dear Claudia,
>
> I am now living in a Christian retirement Community called Carolina Village. My new address is 3025 Cheesbrough Blvd. #218, Rock Hill, SC 29732. Most of the buildings are duplexes. I live in the independent living apartments.

Julia described her rooms and commented on all the "lovely furnishings everywhere." She offered that the people who ran the Community were "fine folks." She then let it all "hang out" about her health, yet with a bit of whimsy.

> I am struggling with diabetes. Also the move here has upset my blood sugar terribly. I found a good internist who increased my insulin and am much better. However, my left knee is a bummer and keeps me from walking since I should exercise for my heart. This gives me no trouble in spite of my doctor who warned me I'd probably just keel over one day. End of story! I swallow a dozen pills a day, and I hope they are the smart ones and know where to go and what to do.

I still drive my Ford Taurus station wagon. Not too much, I'll admit, but it's there when I need it. There is a super Wal-Mart just six miles up the road in S.C. in a green tree-filled state with gentle, soft-spoken people. I'm lonely sometimes when I think of family who are no longer in my life. I'm glad I'm a reader. At the moment, I am finishing Katharine Graham's autobiography, over 500 pages of good writing!

Love ya, *Julia*

Dr. Earl Palmer, former pastor of University Presbyterian Church, Seattle, once said:

The mystery of faith is the Holy Spirit's confirmation that assures the believer, who is en-route in their journey, of deciding whether to trust God or not.

During the last weeks of her journey, Julia, as she had done throughout her long life, exercised one last great act of faith and trust for which she was totally dependent on God. In February 2001, she was one of nineteen Wycliffe colleagues who moved into the relatively new Carolina Village in Rock Hill, South Carolina.[28] One friend was Ruth Bishop, who, in an amazing step of faith and appreciation for history, saved most of Julia's letters, from which I have drawn Julia's story. Another longtime friend and colleague was Olga Warner Penzin. Olga was a co-worker with Julia

---

[28] This is now called Park Pointe Village

in 1957 and it was she who wrote and told me about an amazing answer to Julia's prayer:

"One afternoon I visited Julia, who was then in the Assisted Living section of Carolina Village. When I knocked on her door and opened it, I heard her faintly call, 'Come in.' Julia had a problem speaking as her words or phrases come out on little puffs of air. Besides this, a loose cough sometimes interrupted her speech. The sun was shining brightly through her window that looked out on a pleasant back lawn, with shrubbery below her window and along a back fence. Julia was lying in bed, covered with a pretty quilt. In a few moments she said, 'Did you hear about my big answer to prayer?' Although she had some difficulty speaking, none of this kept her from telling me her story:

> You know I have to take a lot of medicine, twelve pills a day, and my medicine is very expensive. The result is that I have a debt to the Carolina Village pharmacy of $2000.00, and I didn't know how I could pay it. Then one day while I was wondering how I would ever get such a large amount of money I received a phone call. It was from a Mr. O'Connor in Oklahoma, who said he would like to buy the mineral rights on some property in Oklahoma.
>
> You know all about the Oklahoma land rush of 1889. Well, my grandparents were part of that great rush for land. My grandmother just stepped over the state line from Arkansas into

Oklahoma and grabbed some land right there. And my grandfather got another piece of land. Together they had 160 acres. Later oil was found on their land, enough that a rail line was laid out to get to it. For a while, the land gave up its reserve of oil, and then the oil became much less. After my grandparents died, the mineral rights were passed on to my grandparent's descendants. My cousins received portions, and I got my share.

While I was in Mexico, I would occasionally receive a check for twenty-five dollars or some smaller amount. And then those checks stopped coming. The rail line that went to the property was torn up. The soil down deep is oily, but not concentrated enough to draw oil out. So this Mr. O'Connor, who called me, said he wanted to buy the mineral rights and develop the property. So I told him, I'm nearly eighty-five years old and not well, and haven't any use for the property, so I might as well sell.

"Julia went on to tell how she received documents from Mr. O'Connor for her to sign before a notary public. She could do that right at Carolina Village. When Mr. O'Conner returned the signed documents, there was a check for over two-thousand dollars. When she received the check Julia, laughing with satisfaction, said:

I immediately wrote a check for two thousand dollars to pay the pharmacy, and I had some money left over. Here at the last days of my life God has once again been faithful and has answered my prayers in a way I could have never dreamed.

"As I turned to leave I noticed that her room contained several packing boxes and stacks of neatly folded clothing. The floor around one chair showed evidence of sorting. While she never mentioned it directly to me, it was clear she sensed the end of her earthly life was drawing to a close. She did say she had called her niece to see if she would like some of her special keepsakes. As I turned to leave that afternoon, I noticed a photo of Julia's husband alongside a photo of a much younger Julia. That was the last time I saw her. Julia went to be with the Lord she had served so faithfully on December 15, 2004."

The notice of Julia's death appeared in the Friday December 17, 2004 edition of the Enquire-Journal. In short, bare-bones sentences it read:

Julia Andrus WAXHAW

Julia Helen Supple Andrus, 85, died Wednesday (December 15, 2004) at Carolina Village Assisted Living in Rock Hill, S.C. Funeral arrangements are incomplete and will be announced by Davis Funeral and Cremation Service.

When I first read this notice, I thought how very unfair. It was almost obscene to conclude the life of such a valiant and faithful servant of God with such a matter-of-fact six line obituary. But then I realized that this really wasn't the end of Julia's journey. As J.B. Phillips has written: *"If we believe in both what Christ said and what he demonstrated, what we call death is only the gateway to something more splendid and glorious than what we at present imagine."*[29]

And then, from the authority of Romans 8:35-39, William Barclay reminds us: *"Nothing can separate us from Christ's love. Death is not the end it's only the gate on the skyline leading to the presence of Christ."*

Julia Helen Supple Andrus's new life was just beginning.

---

[29] J.B. Phillips, *For This Day* (Waco, Texas, Word Books 1974), p. 63.

Afterword

Outside Help

In her May-June 1960 "Aaron and Hur" letter, Julia candidly admitted that the job of translating the New Testament into Tojolabal and establishing an indigenous church was, for her, an impossible task without "outside help." Such help came in 1976, just as Julia was about to take on a new role as the surrogate mother to Panchita in Southern California.

That year the Reformed Church in America assigned Canadians Chris and Henny Platteel to work among the Tojolabal people. Before building their own house in the village of Santa Lucia, the Platteels lived in Las Margaritas, and with Julia's blessing, in the house she had vacated. With a new Reformed mission partnership, Julia was hopeful this young energetic and eager couple would complete what she had left undone. However, after six years of service and the tragic death of two of their infant children from a congenital disease, Chris and Henny returned to their home in Canada.

Then Sam and Helen Hofman, gifted and dedicated

Reformed Church missionaries, felt called to leave the well-established highly-successful work among the Tzeltals to fill the vacuum left by the Platteels.[30] After the Platteels left the field, Sam was concerned for the ongoing work among the Tojolabals. With this concern came the growing conviction that God was leading them to fill that vacuum. However, their decision to leave the Tzeltals and work among the Tojolabals came only after a great deal of prayer, soul searching, and advice from friends, family and colleagues. Helen had concerns about their physical health and learning a new and difficult language as older workers. They were due to retire in about twelve years.

But then came several tipping points that helped them reach their decision. One came when Sam, with occasional help from Helen, completed a survey of the Tojolabal area to determine just how many evangelical believers there were among the Tojolabal. From her spiritual journal, Helen wrote:

> To Sam's utter delight, he and his survey team kept running into small clusters of believers. In one area, they found a congregation of about 150 with several young men acting as leaders in spite of little or no teaching from the Bible. One of the most promising villages was Benito

---

[30] Sam and Helen had met Julia in 1958 when, as new missionaries, they were studying Spanish in Mexico City. Later, when Julia was nearing retirement from the field, Sam asked Julia if she would welcome Reformed missionaries to continue the work she had begun. Julia was delighted when the Platteels were assigned to the Tojolabals.

Juárez, where a congregation had been formed under the leadership of Alberto Gomez, a Tzeltal medical evangelist. North of Benito Juárez, Tzeltals in the village of Chapayal had built a large stone church that rose out of the jungle like an ancient Mayan pyramid. Under their pastoral care were six thriving Tojolabal congregations in surrounding villages.

In yet another area, the people told Sam all the New Testaments Julia Supple had translated were gone, and they were asking for more. In one small village, just as Sam and his team happened by, the people wanted Sam and his team to show them how to have Christian burial.

Several months after this survey, Helen was reading the first chapter of the book of Joshua and read verse 9: "*Be strong and courageous. Don't be terrified, do not be discouraged, for the Lord your God will be with you wherever you go.*" In her journal, Helen wrote:

> I knew these words were directed to Joshua after God had appointed him to take the place of Moses after he had died. However, as I read those words, they seemed also to be directed to me. Then our mission board asked us to gather further information about the need for someone to help the Tojolabals. A bit later we received an unexpected letter. The letter was typewritten and signed by eleven Christian Tojolabal groups in

the area of Las Margaritas, asking if we would please come and help them to learn more of God's Word. They said they needed help in their own language.

That was all the convincing Sam and Helen and their mission board needed. In January 1988, Sam and Helen moved to Las Margaritas where for the next six years they served the Tojolabals by preparing Bible study materials and training church leaders. They requested a reprint of the Tojolabal New Testament and began distribution of the 5,000 copy edition. In addition, they taught music and expanded the Tojolabal hymnal. One of the first things the Hofmans discovered was that the women were singing hymns in Spanish but did not understand the words. They wanted hymns in their own heart language.

One of the unexpected activities that occupied the Hofman's energies was ministering to the growing number of persecuted Tojolabal believers, which had continued from Julia's time. Although, as noted previously, Mexico legally recognizes freedom of religion, in some villages, if people openly declare themselves to be evangelical Christians, the village elders force them to leave. In two cases among the Tojoloabal, groups of new believers gathered together to form their own villages.

During their six-year tenure among the Tojolabals, the Hofmans recognized the need for a translation of the Old Testament. But, as they admitted, they did not have either the fluency in the Tojolabal language or the time with all of their other duties to undertake such an exhausting project.

Thus, in 1994, the Hofmans left the work in the hands of new Reformed Church missionaries, Brian and Donna Renes, and returned to work again among the Tzeltals.

Unfortunately, after a five-year term, the Reneses, because of the ill health of their daughter, were forced to leave the field. However, Brian periodically continues to be engaged in the Tojolabal work. As a translation consultant for the United Bible Society, he has been eager to encourage Tojolabal Bible translation. In March 2011, he wrote:

> There is a dedicated team of young Tojolabal men who are involved in the revision of the Tojolabal Old and New Testaments. To date, about one-third of the Old Testament has been drafted and about half of the New Testament has been revised. In my work with the Reformed Church, I help them from time to time, but I do not live there full time. I support a variety of projects in the region and can only visit the project a few times a year. The Tojolabal translators received training in translation principles through a program developed by the United Bible Societies and SIL. The program is three months of training spread over three years.

As this book neared completion, Brian wrote the following: "I was with the Tojolabals about three times this year and this last time in August [2012], I worked with a pastor and his son who are adding to the Tojolabal hymnal.

Julia helped them with about 50 or 60 hymns and over the years they continued to add a few more. In the past couple of years they have worked hard to translate even more and now have about 150 hymns. I am always blessed by spending time with them."

It's clear from Scripture that the Holy Spirit is the one who brings people into the Kingdom of God and equips them with gifts and talents to be used for God's glory. For Julia, her gift and responsibility among the Tojolabal was to plough and sow and translate the Good Seed of the gospel. She was then to have the patience of the farmer and wait for the harvest. But like many who do the hard work of preparing the ground for the seed to take root, they can sometimes lose heart that anything will come of their effort.

Such was the case with Julia after her New Testament had been published. For a short time in 1973, Julia lived at the SIL translation center in Mitla, Oaxaca. Living next door to Julia were Ted and Kris Jones, a new SIL couple then in the process of deciding what language group God would have them serve. One day Kris saw Julia and said to her, "You must be thrilled to have finished your New Testament." To Kris's surprise Julia said:

> No not really, I doubt if anyone will read it, except my language helper, maybe. The Branch wanted me to get it printed, but I am afraid it will just sit in some storage area and get moldy.

She, of course, was not the first or last person to feel this way. Long ago Isaiah said to God, "*I have labored to no purpose; I have spent my strength in vain and for nothing"* (Isaiah 49:4).

What Julia may have forgotten is that it takes some seeds longer to germinate than others. Fortunately, Julia lived long enough to learn that some of the good seed had blossomed into the lives of clusters of believers who were eager to read the New Testament for themselves. Sadly, what she never did learn was what SIL colleagues Kris Jones and Mary Benton communicated to me about a young man named Pedro Hernández Jiménez.

Pedro was one of five siblings who, at about age fifteen after hearing the gospel for several weeks, declared his intention to become a follower of Jesus Christ. And like many new believers, he endured opposition from his immediate family, particularly his father. So opposed was his father to his son's commitment to Christ that he confiscated Pedro's Bible and notebooks. And to prevent him from attending church, he made Pedro work in the family's cornfields on Sunday. But in spite of these interruptions, Pedro remained faithful and continued to share his faith with his family and to pray that God would make them receptive to God's sacrificial love as found in the person of His Son Jesus Christ. In God's providence, each of Pedro's siblings and his mother confessed their faith in Jesus Christ.

After Pedro graduated from high school, he took a position as a bilingual (Spanish and Tojolabal) elementary school teacher. After a year of teaching, Pedro began thinking about going to the university to study engineering. But one day while visiting his pastor, Pedro said he wanted to "serve God in a good way." Pedro's pastor suggested he check out a special workshop sponsored by SIL on Bible translation principles.

When Pedro learned there was a three-week workshop in Mitla, Oaxaca, and that there was an opportunity for him to begin revision of the Tojolabal New Testament, he jumped at the chance. Pedro was an eager student, did well in the course and continued to upgrade his skills by taking advanced courses.

At one of these workshops, Pedro's teacher was Joaquín, who had been the co-translator with Ted Jones as they worked on the Guelavía Zapotec New Testament. Joaquín now serves as a consultant to other indigenous translators and teaches at workshops. Pedro asked Joaquín for his help and both are now part of a dedicated team working on the revision of the Tojolabal New Testament.

There is often a gap between promise and fulfillment. And although it took longer than Julia Supple Andrus would have liked, God's promise that His Word would not return void of a harvest has come true for many Tojolabals. In Pedro's town, for example, there are thirteen evangelical churches and the Tojolabal New Testament is read in many of their church services. Although these churches represent several different denominations, they are friendly to each other. What's more, there is now an evangelical witness in most of the Tojolabal communities.

Julia's May-June 1960 letter had expressed her desire for an extended partnership from folks at home and colleagues on the field who possessed different skill sets for ministry. In the letter, Julia once more emphasized her own priorities, namely, "Getting the Word of God translated into Tojolabal, the only language they really comprehend." In God's time, the "outside" help she prayed for came from the Reformed Church colleagues. And in God's time, building on Julia's foundation, they could report that there are now an estimated 5,000 to 10,000 baptized Tojolabal believers.

> We are one body in Christ,
> We have different gifts.
> according to the grace
> that has been given to us,
> Let's use them in mutual service.
> (Romans 12:3-5, William Barclay paraphrase.)

At her core, Julia Supple Andrus was an optimist. In her heart and mind, she knew that God was the God of all things. She thus was certain that in spite of hardships, persecutions, interferences, misunderstandings, lack of finances, ill health and even death, the "best was yet to be." As she often reminded her correspondents throughout her life:

> I am not afraid of tomorrow
> For I've seen yesterday
> And I love today.

Acknowledgments

It was Ulysses, in the Alfred, Lord Tennyson poem of the same name, who said, "*I am part of all that I have met.*" And this is never truer than for of a writer of biographies. I therefore acknowledge my heartfelt thanks and gratefulness to God for my wife, Norma, who is my indispensable partner and best friend in our writing ministry with Wycliffe Bible Translators. Norma acted as my editor for this book, as she has done for most of my other books.

I am also grateful for the many friends, colleagues and acquaintances we have met over these past fifty years who have contributed, knowingly and unknowingly, to the great tapestry of our lives. Norma and I owe an incredible debt of thanks to our prayer and financial supporters who have made it possible for our continued ministry with Wycliffe. I am especially grateful to Don and Leone Woods, longtime friends, for their generous financial support for this book project. I also here thank Barbara Wylie and the Trinity United Presbyterian Church prayer group in Santa Ana, Cailifornia. Because of their enduring prayer partnership, they have shared equally in whatever influence and encouragement my books have been to the body of Christ. According to Scripture, there are rich rewards for them laid up in heaven for safe keeping.

I owe a special thank you to Wycliffe Archivist, Cal Hibbard, longtime friend and colleague and instigator on a number of my writing projects. It was his continued persistence that I should examine Julia's letters. "They are pure gold and should be mined," he said. I am also indebted to Ruth Bishop, also a longtime friend and colleague from our days together in Mexico. She discovered the letters after Julia had died and sent them to Cal Hibbard for safekeeping. "They are just too good to be discarded," she said.

I am grateful to Dale Barkley, Executive Secretary for the Mexico Branch of SIL, who went the second mile and photocopied a number of Julia's primary documents and extra letters that were indispensable in understanding her story. I thank him also for his warm personal encouragement to write the story. Also to Ron Newberg, Director of the Mexico Branch of SIL, who, like Dale, gave me his blessing and warm encouragement to bring Julia's story to life. Also from the Mexico Branch, I am particularly grateful to Mae Toedter, who came out of retirement and acted as editor and checker of all facts as related to the Mexico Branch. If there are any oversights or errors, the faults are mine alone.

I am grateful to Olga Warner Penzin, former SIL colleague and friend from Mexico, for sharing the poignant story of her last visit with Julia. To Marianna Slocum, also an SIL colleague and longtime friend, for her historical memo on Julia's New Testament. Also, I here thank Kris Jones and Mary Benton, SIL colleagues, for their generous help in bringing me up-to-date on the Tojolabal New Testament revision and allowing me to use Pedro's story.

A special word of appreciation is due to Reformed Church missionaries and friends of many years, Sam and Helen Hofman. They filled in many blanks in Julia's story, as did Brian and Donna Renes. They especially helped me to understand the growth of the Tojolabal Church after Julia's retirement.

I thank Valerie Stevenson, a longtime friend and my former secretary who worked with Julia in Wycliffe's Huntington Beach Editorial Department and remembered the details surrounding Julia's engagement and wedding.

To Julia's niece, Mrs. Claudia Cowan, I owe a special word of appreciation for supplying me with old photos and having the foresight to save some of Julia's most insightful letters, including her last hand-written letter from the care home.

I here thank Jewel Fink, friend and former Wycliffe colleague, for her creative cover design and enthusiasm for the project. Thanks to my son-in-law, Greg Asimakou-poulos for his photo of me on the back cover. My grateful thanks and appreciation also go to my son, Lee, who chose the type and internal book design, formatted the book for publication, and offered his support and literary skill in the final edit.

Finally, I thank Dr. Helen Guillen, resident of Comitán, Mexico and Julia's long-time friend. Dr. Guillen remembers

Julia for her many kindnesses and thoughtful gifts that she gave to her landlady when Julia returned from a tip to the States. Said Dr. Guillen, "I recall that in spite of her busy schedule, Julia always remembered birthdays and special details about a person's life. She was a blessing to all who knew her."

Appendix A

Idiomatic Translations

In my book, *The John Beekman Story, The Man With the Noisy Heart,* John Beekman explains how a translator must be aware of collocational clashes, that is, words that go together in English but not in another language. The word *run* presents a common example. In English, a river can run, a boy can run, a fox can run. One's nose can run, as can a car. However, in some languages only a boy can run.

And consider the verse where Jesus says that a "house divided against itself shall not stand" (Matt. 12:25). In English, we know what this figure of speech means. It refers to the people in or of the house, not to the physical structure. But some languages cannot refer to people as a house, nor can people be divided. They may be against each other, but only a person literally cut in half is divided. The same is true of the verse in Genesis where we are told that God divided light from darkness. In some languages, darkness is not divisible; you cannot cut it. It is therefore crucial to avoid collocational clashes creeping into one's translation if one wants to produce a meaningful, readable text.

Then, of course, there is the problem of how to express abstract nouns and difficult words like *sanctification*, *love*, *hope*, and *justification*. In a language in Peru, the translator had a problem with the word *world* from John 3:16 because the closest equivalent in the language referred only to the dirt, and the translator didn't want to say that "God loved the dirt or ground." The translator found that the clearest expression was to say, "this earth here, those from," which, more freely translated, means "all people."

In Mark 12, we are told to beware of scribes who devour widows' houses. In many tropical cultures, the only things that eat palm houses are animals or jungle termites. Thus, the indigenous person could only conclude that a scribe is either an animal or an insect. A similar problem occurs in Luke 13:32, where Jesus calls Herod a fox. In some languages, this expression used in this context refers to a homosexual. In others it means one who cries too much, and in still others it means one who steals. Thus, it is not possible simply to translate word for word. Equivalents in the target language must be found to convey, as clearly as possible, the full meaning of the original.

Martin Luther understood the importance of using the right expression in translation. His supreme desire was to place the Word of God into the hands of the people because, he said, "*Here was where they would find Jesus Christ. The holy scripture is the cradle in which Christ is laid.*"

The goal of an idiomatic Bible translation is to express

the meaning of the original scriptures in the most natural, elegant and effective way possible in the target language. The translation must remain faithful to the original text while also being true to the syntactical and lexical forms unique to the language into which the Bible is to be translated.

Appendix B

An Explanation of "Aaron and Hur"

The story of Aaron and Hur begins in Exodus 17:8-16 when Israel faced yet another crisis of war. This time the conflict was with Israel's cousins, the Amalekites.[31] The issue was over pastoral land and Israel was threatened with an invasion by a large company of people. Complicating the matter was Israel's desire for retribution against the Amalekites for attacking defenseless stragglers leaving Egypt (see Deuteronomy 25:17).

When war became inevitable, Moses, now too old to fight, chose Joshua to "do battle against the Amalekites." He retired with Aaron and Hur (prominent members of the council of elders) to higher ground where they had a stadium view of the battle. It was here that Moses promised

---

[31] I am indebted to Bernard L. Ramm for his book, *His Way Out, A Fresh Look at Exodus*, published by Regal Books, Glendale, California, 1952, for insights into this passage.

to hold the staff of God above his head for all to see and take courage.

The staff, or rod, with perhaps Israel's banner on it, was a sign of God's strength, God's power and God's enablement. It was a promise of victory. However, if the staff dropped, it meant that the warriors of Israel would be fighting in their own strength and that they would became discouraged and not prevail.

The lesson that Julia wanted to stress was that, just as Aaron and Hur held up Moses' arms when he became tired, and thus were, in fact, a necessary part of Israel's victory, so, too, she needed "Aarons and Hurs" to support her and do spiritual battle so that the Church of God would prevail among the Tojolabal people. Julia knew that hers was a task too large and too important for one person. She needed the support of praying partners, whom she called "Aaron and Hur," to share the burden and responsibility of giving a people God's Word in their own language.

Made in the USA
Charleston, SC
03 December 2012